G000048921

Remember Me?

a memoir

Mary Monaghan

TORTOISE
PRESS

First published 2006 by Tortoise Press,
P O Box 163, Melkbosstrand 7437, South Africa
www.marymonaghan.com

Second Edition 2007

ISBN 978-0620-36648-9

Printed and bound by MegaDigital
Cover from an original painting by Osnat

For my parents, Kathryn, and Annie
who have always been there for me

Acknowledgements

This book would never have been written without the help of so many special people. I owe an immense debt to Anne Schuster for her positive guidance and to Romaine Hill for her meticulous and motivating editing. To Bridgett Whyte, Jan Glazewski, Cheryl Leslie, Jean Green and Nicole Chidrawi who read and reread my drafts and always provided great encouragement, I am forever grateful.

Then to my friends, many of whom appear in these pages, for encouraging me to write my story and helping me to follow my dream. My life has always been enriched by your friendship. Special thanks to Nigel in Ireland, Deirdre, Lynn, Margaret, Pam, Peter and Wendy in Johannesburg, to Diane, Linda, Yvette, Ann, Jenny, Joan and Terry in Cape Town, and to my neighbours in Grotto Bay, Nicky and Gerald, who respected the space I needed to write.

# Contents

Leaving for Australia 1

Meeting in London 11

Courtship 19

Wedding 27

Birthday wishes 39

Chicken farming 45

Steve's funeral 51

Airport 55

Christmas 59

Interpol 63

New beginnings 69

Grotto Bay 77

Nigel's revelations 87

Mother's death 95

Crisis of faith 101

Annulment 109

Gorilla trekking 117

Old friends 127

Granny's funeral 137

Journey's end 143

Remember me?

Remember me?
I am your wife
Creating your home
Cooking your meals
Washing your clothes
Unfulfilled, dependant
And stifled, stifled

Remember me?
I am your wife
Your deserted wife
Waiting, longing
Weeping, hoping
Your vulnerable wife
Your needy wife

Remember me?
No longer your wife
Creating my home
Feeding my spirit
Living my dream
Fulfilled and independent
And alive, alive

I am the woman
You never knew
Free, strong and passionate
I am the woman
You never knew
Remember me?

Leaving for Australia

'I don't want you to see me off at the airport,' John's tone had an air of finality to it; he wasn't going to accept any argument. 'I don't want to remember you being upset as you wave me off. I want to rather see your smiling face when I get back.'

'But I can't let you go without saying goodbye properly.'

'We'll say goodbye at the house, it will be better that way.'

On and off over the next few days I attempted to change his mind, but with no success. I resigned myself to the fact that I wasn't going to the airport with him. It was hard to believe that only three months had gone by since he had broken the news to me, in November 1992:

'I want to close the company and take some time out for myself as soon as the contract in Richards Bay is finished. I'll go backpacking in Australia for three months. Once I have recharged my batteries we can start up something else. I just need to get away for a bit to clear my head, then I'll be ready to start again.'

It all made a lot of sense to me. He had started his industrial painting company eight years ago and spent most of that time working long hours in godforsaken places, all over the country, getting out of it only stress and aggravation. It had never been easy, but lately it was a constant battle to get payments in on time to keep both staff and creditors happy. He deserved a break; the strain was starting to take its toll on him. Signs of stress lined his face and there was only a hint of his usual smile. He was drinking heavily, becoming aggressive and was prone to sudden mood swings. This wasn't the John I knew.

'I know we don't have a lot of money,' he said, 'so I won't keep in too much contact. I'll use my Diner's Club card so you'll see where I am and that I am ok.'

I took a deep breath. Logically, I knew all of this made sense but it scared me.

'I don't want anyone to know that I am going to Australia otherwise they will think I am considering emigrating, which I'm not. I'm going to tell them I am going to Mozambique to do contract work, that way they won't wonder what I am up to.'

I agreed to go with his story, but was uncomfortable at the deception. Why couldn't we just be honest with everyone? I thought to myself.

I knew we would struggle financially and was prepared for that. He had to go; he was close to burn-out. His phone calls to me from Richards Bay had become sporadic. I couldn't be sure but it felt like he was starting to distance himself from me, preparing me for his months away.

'We will have to sell the house. It will give us enough money to buy another one which needs renovating, then I'll do it up for resale. I can work on my own, no staff problems and it will give us a good income. You can put the house on the market while I'm away and look for another one for me to renovate when I get back.'

I swallowed hard; I didn't want him to see the tears welling in my eyes. I loved our house; it wasn't anything special but it was home and had been for seven years. We moved in just after we were married and it held many happy memories, but if we had to move, so be it.

John was not going to change his mind about going away, that was clear. I knew I had to make the most of what was going to happen and support him in his plan. There were three months before he left anyway, but in the months leading up to his departure we did not see that much of each other. He was finishing off the contract in Richards Bay and was working long hours and most weekends so he had very little opportunity to come home to Mondeor before Christmas. He would be leaving in early February, so time was short.

We planned to have our usual Christmas lunch at home; we always invited friends to join us. It was traditionally a noisy, happy occasion and I was determined that this time would be no different. I wanted it to be special, as he would be leaving for Australia soon. I shopped for all the goodies to make it a special day, crackers, fun gifts for everyone and of course the food: turkey, gammon, Christmas pudding, mince pies, not to mention Champagne, wine, whiskey. I loved the preparations; it was all part of the build up. I made sure I had presents for everyone, even those who were last-minute additions. Nigel would join us of course. I don't think he had ever missed a Christmas with us. Nigel had been a part of our lives since we first arrived in South Africa. He was Irish, from Cork, a plumber by trade and almost the same age as John.

Christmas Eve morning arrived. John was still not home; it had been a few days since I had heard from him. I went to the post box to collect the mail, plenty of Christmas cards and the Diner's Club statement. I checked out the charges, just one stood out, an air ticket to South America; the passenger name, 'Miss T Riekert'. Who could that be? The name sounded familiar, I couldn't work out why. I picked up the phone and called Robbie Sharpe, our travel agent.

'It is the correct charge,' he said.

'But who is the passenger?' I asked.

'A friend of John's,' he replied.

I went cold, battling to breathe, what was this all about I asked myself?

'I think you should ask John about it, I'm sorry I can't give you any more details.'

I struggled to maintain my composure. 'Of course,' I replied, not wanting Robbie to see how upset I was. 'I'll speak to him later, thanks for your help.'

'I'm sorry Mary,' he said, as the line went dead.

I paced around the garden, trying to make sense of what I had just heard. What was going on? I repeated the name over and over, why did it ring such a bell? Of course, that's right, I thought, I've seen it on a cheque. I ran back into the house and rummaged in the filing drawer. There they were, several cheques made out to cash with the name 'Riekert' written on the back. John had always maintained they were for supplies, obviously not.

Still no sign of John, the excitement of Christmas Eve was turning into apprehension. But I knew he would arrive at the last minute as usual and then we would make our annual pilgrimage to Sandton City. True to form he phoned from the airport that afternoon.

'Hello sweetheart, I'm here, please come and fetch me, then let's go shopping.'

I dashed to the airport, knowing that we would need to hurry around the shops before closing time.

John's face lit up in a wide grin as I drew up outside the arrivals hall. 'Bet you thought that I wouldn't make it in time!' he said.

'Oh, I knew you would,' I replied, happy that he was home but disconcerted to see that he had been drinking heavily again. This was happening too frequently these days. I couldn't have the conversation about the air ticket with him now, he was almost incoherent. It would serve no purpose.

And so we set off for our annual shopping spree. It wasn't too late when we got home and I started preparing the vegetables for the next day. It was all part of my routine; I played the tape of King's College Choir, *Carols from King's*, and thought of my mother. It had been her Christmas ritual to prepare the vegetables every Christmas Eve at 3 p.m. as carols from King's was broadcast on BBC radio. I continued the tradition and kept her in my thoughts as I did.

We went to bed early but tossed and turned. We both knew that there was something wrong, but the time wasn't right to address it. We had all our friends arriving for Christmas and had to make sure they enjoyed themselves.

Christmas lunch was long and festive as usual. I loved being surrounded by friends. It was always a day full of fun and laughter, but this Christmas was so different. It was soured by my apprehension about John's going away and the uncertainty of what the next three months would hold, not to mention the revelation of the previous day and what that meant. We smiled and joked as usual but it was all show. I tried to block everything out and enjoy the moment, but it wasn't that easy. Eventually everyone left except for Nigel. He always stayed until Boxing Day, and we settled down to relax and watch some videos. He had known us long enough to feel the tension in the air and soon excused himself, going to sleep in the guest cottage at the bottom of the garden.

Now was my chance to speak to John. I just hadn't been able to confront him before. Once Nigel was out of earshot, we had our privacy. I showed him the Diner's Club statement. 'Robbie says this person is a friend of yours.'

He went pale. 'Sweetheart, I'm so sorry. I wanted to tell you, I just didn't know how.'

'Tell me now,' I replied as the tears ran freely down my cheeks. 'Who is she? What is going on?'

'She's a friend of mine. I met her when Jimmy and I went hiking in the Drakensberg, the time you and Kathryn went to Cyprus after your mother died.'

'But that was 1989, over three years ago.'

Then it all came out. He told me how he had been living with Tracey when he was working in Richards Bay, how they had been renovating a house together in the East Rand. She even attended work functions with him. His travelling around the country working on contracts made it all so easy.

I sobbed uncontrollably, 'I thought you loved me.'

'I do, I love you so much.'

'Then how can you do this to me?'

'I don't know, it just happened, I didn't mean for it to be like this. I thought it would be over by now. I can't choose between you. That's why I need to get away, to clear my head; I'm just so confused. I'm sending her to South America, for three months too, so there will be no contact with her either.'

'Great, so you both go swanning off around the world while I just keep the home fires burning,' I retorted, furious at the way everything had been worked out.

How could I be so stupid, why didn't I see the signs? I said to myself. John's behaviour had become increasingly erratic. It had worried me. I had never known him like this, but I had just put it down to the pressures of work, not realising that this was aggravated by the pressure of leading a double life. I felt like a sleepwalker, out of touch with the real world. Everything I had relied on had been turned upside down. I had always been so certain of John's love for me, that had always been the one thing I could depend on. He said he loved me, but how could he if he had done this to me?

We had arranged for Nigel to drop us at the airport a few days later as we had booked to spend New Year at The Polana hotel in Mozambique. We had visited it some months earlier and had fallen in love with its elegance and feel of colonial splendour. It seemed like a good place to see in New Year 1993.

We were only going to be there for three days but as usual my case was packed to overflowing. There was a dinner dance planned for New Year's Eve and I had bought a beautiful dress for the occasion. When I had seen it in the shop window I had instantly fallen in love with it, but was more than aware that it was figure hugging and unlikely to look too good on my frame. I took the plunge and decided to try it on, I wasn't too hopeful as I knew the limitations of my figure only too well. To my amazement, it fitted, not only that, it was actually too big! I asked the assistant to find me one in a smaller size and, to my surprise, it fitted perfectly. It was only then I realised how much weight I had lost as the strain of John's betrayal and his imminent departure took their toll.

We arrived at the airport in Maputo and the heat and humidity enveloped us. Our clothes stuck to us and our faces were glistening with a thin layer of perspiration. It was far hotter than when we had last been there in August. We had done all the tours on our previous trip so were content to laze around the hotel pool and walk into town to visit the local restaurants. We tried to relax but there was an unmistakable tension between us. We were trying hard to ignore the fact that this would be our last trip together for a while and were trying to make it seem as normal as possible, but there was no doubt we were both feeling the pressure. I knew, too, that when he came back it would by no means be plain sailing. There was so much unfinished business. He was going to Australia, Tracey was going to South America and I was going absolutely nowhere.

New Year's Eve arrived. I changed into my beautiful new dress, applied my make up in the bathroom and emerged to parade in front of John. He glanced up from the magazine he was reading, a look of appreciation in his eyes, 'Wow, you look incredible. Amazing.'

Then an acknowledgement of the strain he had put me under. 'I didn't realise how much weight you had lost; I've never seen you so thin.'

It was true, I looked fabulous but was almost unhealthily thin, and I wasn't built to be too skinny. If I lost any more weight I would start looking haggard. We decided to take photos in the room before we left for dinner in all our finery. We looked great but I still couldn't shift the hollow feeling in my heart. I wanted a record of our New Year together, and made sure we took some photos. We were going through the motions, attempting to enjoy ourselves but we weren't fooling anyone, least of all ourselves. We ate a sumptuous dinner in the ballroom; the setting was exquisite, crystal glasses, red and white table settings, and red roses. The food was spectacular, rare roast fillet of beef, prawns and baked Alaska for dessert. Once dinner was over, we danced around the pool, to the sounds of the band, toasting in the New Year with French champagne before going back to our room. I burst into tears as we wished each other Happy New Year, I couldn't keep up the pretence any more.

I turned to John as we lay in bed and said, 'This probably wasn't the best idea; we should have stayed at home.'

'I wanted it to be special for you,' he replied.

'How can it be? It can never be special again.' We had always been so happy together; he loved me, so how could he be living a double life?

He held me tight, 'It will be all right, we'll work it out. I don't want to lose you.'

I so wanted to believe him, but I couldn't stop the feeling of foreboding that was constantly with me. I went into 1993 with a heavy heart, knowing it was going to be a trying year. Even the New Year's Eve photos of us at The Polana hadn't come out, nothing seemed to be going right.

A month went by and I tossed and turned that February night, lying in bed, trying to sleep, listening to the sound of cars in the distance. John was leaving the next day, I wanted the last hours before he left to be happy ones but I just couldn't settle. I finally decided to get up and fetch a glass of water from the kitchen, maybe that would help. I stubbed my toe on the armchair as I made for the door, letting out a cry of pain.

'Are you all right, sweetheart?' John asked, woken by the noise.

'I'm fine, just thirsty.'

'Come back to bed.'

I slid under the duvet; he turned over and cuddled me. 'It's going to be ok, I promise, try to sleep now.'

But would it, I thought. How could it ever be ok again?

I snuggled into the warmth of his body and eventually managed to doze off. All too soon the clock radio announced the new day. I had to go to work, life was going to carry on as usual today, same routines, just one thing was going to be different. When I got home, John wasn't going to be there. He would be on his way to Sydney.

'I'll make you some coffee,' he said to me as I showered.

'That will be nice,' I responded, wondering how I was going to be able to get it down my throat. An overwhelming sense of panic mingled with a violent nausea gripped me. How was I ever going to get through this day? Be strong I told myself, you don't want John's last picture of you to be that of a hysterical, snivelling female. I was determined to look my best so that his last memory of me would be a good one. I got out of the shower, dried myself off and padded to the bedroom to get dressed and dry my hair. I had had my hair cut a few weeks before and it was really looking good. I smiled at the mirror; despite everything, I wasn't looking too bad. I went to the wardrobe and picked out the blue and pink floral suit that John liked so much. I was pulling out all the stops today. It fitted well, even better than usual, was loose because of the weight I had continued to lose in the last few weeks; stress had some compensation, I thought ruefully. At last I was ready, briefcase packed and dressed smartly. I joined John in the kitchen. He was sitting at the kitchen table staring bleary eyed into the distance as he clutched his early morning cup of coffee.

'Wow, you look beautiful,' a faint smile contrasted with the sadness reflected in his eyes. 'I've made you coffee and toast.'

I sat down, putting the mug of hot coffee to my lips but hardly able to swallow a drop.

He reached for my hand. 'I'll be back soon, it's just three months, it'll go quickly, you'll see.'

I was trying so hard not to cry but I could feel the tears coming. 'I know, I know, but I'm going to miss you so much.'

'I'll be back before you know it.' He leaned over to give me one of his wonderful all-enveloping bear hugs, which always made me feel so safe and loved, only today it wasn't working, I felt shaky and vulnerable. 'Come on, it's time for you to go otherwise you'll be late for work. Give me your briefcase.' He followed me to the car and placed my briefcase in the boot. 'Don't be sad sweetheart, I'll be back soon. I'll phone you before I go to the airport. I love you very much.'

'I love you too,' I said as I got into the car. I lowered the car window and tried to smile bravely as I reversed out of the driveway. I watched John's smile fade as I drove away, unsettled by the image of his grim face. Why had I agreed not to go to the airport? But I had promised and so I must stick to what I had said.

Concentrate, I said to myself as I drove through the rush-hour traffic, the last thing you want to do now is to have an accident. The cars sped by me in a blur and somehow I ended up safely at the office.

It was a beautiful Highveld summer's morning, the kind of morning that would generally make my heart sing, but today all I could think about was making it through the day. We were like a family at work so everyone knew what was happening. I had told them that I wanted things to carry on as normal and they were trying to respect that, but every now and again I could spot them casting furtive glances in my direction, just checking that I was ok.

Nigel was going to drop John off at the airport. He idolised him, regarding him as a role model. Nigel had always been there for both of us, giving up weekends to help us renovate the old farmhouse we had bought outside Magaliesburg, and just generally being there whenever help was needed. He had agreed to be my 'minder' and look after and help me with anything I needed in the three months that John was going to be away. To many people, Nigel was unreliable, spending most of his free time at the pub, smoking and drinking too much and flirting with the girls, but we could always count on him and I really valued his friendship.

I glanced at my watch, almost twelve o'clock. Nigel and John would be leaving soon for the airport. I didn't want to stray too far from my desk; I had to be there for John's phone call. I made a feeble attempt to glance at the papers on my desk but they were just a blur of images.

At long last the phone rang. 'Hi sweetheart, it's me; I'm on my way now.' His voice was thick with emotion: 'Be strong. I'll be back soon, I love you.'

'I love you too,' I responded, holding the phone to my ear long after he had put down.

I felt the walls of the office closing in on me. I have to get out of here, I thought, get some air and walk. Anywhere will do. I knew I was in the middle of central Johannesburg, not the safest place to walk but I needed to get out to calm myself. I stepped out of the lift into the heat of the summer's day and lost myself in the busy streets. The rhythmic pounding of my steps on the pavement started to assist in slowing the pace of my heartbeat. I tried hard to stop myself from crying and after wandering aimlessly for six blocks I began to feel calmer.

John was going to be gone for three months. He had worked away from home for weeks at a time before, what was the big deal? I couldn't put my finger on it but this time I had a strong sense of unease.

Meeting in London

I found myself back at the lobby of our building. I'd get through the rest of the day just as long as everyone carried on as normal. Deep down I knew I really wasn't all right, why was I taking this so hard? I was starting to realise that I had reached a turning point in my life. Three months without John and then what? Time will tell, I said to myself as I pressed the lift button for the third floor. Time to consider my options, could I really forgive and forget? What if he couldn't give her up when he came back? He was my husband I would fight for him. I wasn't going to give up that easily. I knew we were meant to be together.

I thought back to how I had met John in London in 1980. It seemed hard to believe it was more than twelve years ago.

'Have a good trip,' I had said to Kathryn as she got onto the bus outside The Crown Hotel in Cricklewood. A new bus service from London to Galway had started, a coach taking you all the way, using the ferry from Holyhead to Dun Laoghaire.

My sister Kathryn was a teacher at a primary school in London and was lucky enough to have long school holidays. She liked to spend them in Ireland, in Ballinrobe where my parents had both been born. They had grown up there before leaving for England in the 1940s, when my father joined the Royal Air Force. Kathryn treasured her Irish roots and loved to spend all her free time in Ballinrobe.

It was great to have somewhere to call home; the disadvantage of being the children of someone in the forces meant that we did not put down roots in any particular place. We were lucky that my father didn't get posted to too many different places, but still it meant that there were no real constants in our lives in terms of childhood friends and family.

The advantage, of course, was that we got the opportunity to travel. I spent the period when I was six to nine years old living in Nicosia in Cyprus. It was a magical time. Kathryn and I ran free in a warm and sunny climate, and it was there that I developed my love of hot places. We attended the primary school on the base but finished every day at 1 p.m., as we had to be home in the heat of the day. We spent most afternoons playing in the Olympic-sized swimming pool, translating all the games usually played on land to the water, becoming real water babies.

Shortly after we arrived in Cyprus civil war broke out between the Greek and Turkish Cypriots. The United Nations were sent in to act as peacekeepers so my parents counted people of all nationalities among their friends. There were troops from England, Canada, Ireland, Sweden, Denmark and Finland, so I grew up in a totally cosmopolitan environment. The sound of shooting coming from the Kyrenia Mountains in the distance was part of the sounds of the evenings in those first few months and as a child I accepted it as the norm.

'All uniformed personnel to stay in uniform for the duration of the alert. Be prepared to evacuate the island with 24 hours notice. No one is permitted to leave the base until further notice.'

My mother sighed as she glanced at Kathryn and me who had also been listening to the radio. It was December 1963 and we had arrived in Cyprus just a month earlier. We had been looking forward to three years of bliss on this beautiful Mediterranean island. My parents had been there previously in the 1950s and had made many good friends.

They were more than happy to return, it was one of the prized postings to get. Although we had arrived in winter, it felt like summer to us, coming as we did from the wintry damp of Lincolnshire.

I was six years old and soon settled into St Michaels' school which was just a few minutes walk from our bungalow. I simply hopped over the fence at the bottom of the garden and was already on the edge of the school sports field, which was nothing at all like the lush green sports field of an English village school. This one was hard and dusty, but did have the advantage of revealing all sorts of interesting fossils if you took the time to look carefully enough.

I could see my mother was worried. She turned to switch off the radio, the emergency broadcast had finished. 'I'm not in the mood to listen any more,' she sighed 'please tidy up your toys, your father will be home soon. He'll be tired as he's been on duty all night and won't want to be falling over all your dolls.'

But I wasn't listening to my mother; I had taken note of the clear instructions, all uniformed personnel to remain in uniform for the duration of the emergency. The instructions had to be obeyed; I rushed to my bedroom, rifled through the clothes hanging in my wardrobe, desperately searching for my Brownie uniform. They had said I must keep it on until further notice and that was exactly what I would do. I battled to knot my tie, made sure all my badges were straight and then rushed to my mother in the kitchen to see if I passed inspection.

'You look very smart,' she said, grinning. 'But why are you in uniform? Brownies meet on Thursday, not on Tuesday.'

'They said on the radio I must stay in my uniform and that's what I am going to do,' I replied, full of pride that I was playing my part. I went to the veranda, lined up my dolls on the step and waited for my father to come home. I stayed in my uniform for two days and nights, refusing to take it off until the 'all clear' was given.

Kathryn and I loved our time in Cyprus, accepting unquestioningly that there were United Nations troops everywhere, and also that on a seventeen-mile journey to the beach in Kyrenia we would be stopped at six checkpoints, two Greek and four Turkish, it was just a way of life for us. It was quite a change when we moved back to RAF Oakington, just outside Cambridge, where we finished our schooling.

The coach to Ireland eventually departed. I waved goodbye to Kathryn and returned to my flat just down the road. I wasn't able to take leave over the summer period and even if I wanted to, money was tight, so the fare would be a problem. I resigned myself to the fact that I would be spending the summer in London, not the most terrible place to be after all. I was managing a restaurant in South Audley Street, just behind Grosvenor Square. It was fun; I enjoyed the people interaction and the celebrity spotting. Quite a few famous people came through our doors and it was always interesting to watch them in their unguarded moments. Many of them were regulars there, Joan Collins, Ringo Starr, Leonard Cohen, the Bee Gees and Mark Thatcher among them.

I had moved to London in the October of 1979 at the age of twenty-two, having finished my degree in French and Spanish, and had promptly gone to France in search of work, setting my heart on living and working in Biarritz, in South Western France, since I had spent a year there teaching English as part of my degree. I had met great friends there, loving the lifestyle and vowing to go back. I hotfooted back there as soon as my degree was finished, but any attempt to find work became bogged down by the French predilection for red tape and it was impossible to find employment.

Begrudgingly I had returned to England and started working in the restaurant, employment for newly qualified language graduates being in short supply. It was a job at least and allowed me to be independent. I rented a small flat in Cricklewood, just opposite The Galtymore, an Irish club. It was about a ten-minute's walk from Kathryn's place and close to bus routes for work, so it was a good starting point for getting myself established. My college had been further up the road in Hampstead, so I was very familiar with the area. I just didn't have too many friends close by, as they had scattered to all parts of the world after we graduated.

Kathryn would have a long journey ahead of her, only arriving in Ballinrobe the next day. I always preferred plane travel myself. Even at a young age I saved money from holiday jobs and travelled in style, no ferries for me! It was warm and stuffy inside my flat, summer had definitely arrived, and London was still and stifling. I opened all the windows but it didn't make too much difference. I took out the newspaper and caught up with all the news in between watching my elderly landlord potter around his garden, feeding his budgies. I looked to see what was on television, not too much; it was mostly taken up with the Moscow Olympics. Between that and my book I should manage to keep myself busy for the evening. Tomorrow was Sunday and I started work at 11 a.m. I enjoyed the shift work and the fact that I had time off during the week. I liked to be off on Saturday as that was usually my night out.

It would be good to go out tonight, I thought to myself, but I have no one to come with me. I was tempted to go across the road to The Galtymore, where they had show bands playing on a Saturday night. People went there to dance and I had often gone there from college on my own, when my friends hadn't wanted to join me. Once you were inside no one knew that you had come on your own as you rarely stopped dancing and, even if you were with a group of friends, you hardly saw each other all evening.

I found it an easy place to go, the music was good, all the latest hit songs with a slight Country and Western feel. Three sets of fast songs or three slow. If you agreed to dance you were committed to stay with your partner for at least three songs. You were far more selective, choosing your partner carefully, when the slow songs came on. The club only got going after the pubs shut so 11 p.m. was the time to get there. It went on until 2 a.m. and was usually packed with young Irish people working in London (many of them employed as nurses or in construction) and anxious to have a link to their roots. I had never lived in Ireland, but The Galty always gave me a strong sense of being home, of belonging. I loved the music and the dancing and the easy banter over a few drinks.

I hadn't felt so strongly aware of my roots until the anti-Irish sentiment of the late 1970s. While I was at college there had been terrorist activity in Northern Ireland, bombs and hunger strikes were the order of the day. In college I was probably one of very few people with Irish roots. Each day the newspaper was full of information on bomb blasts, mostly in Northern Ireland but now we were having bomb scares in London too.

One day a group of us were going to the West End to see a play but suddenly all my friends wanted to cancel. 'It's too dangerous,' they said. 'What if there's a bomb?' There had been several bomb scares in the last few days.

I was pragmatic, a great believer in fate, 'If it is meant to be, it is meant to be, I'm still going to go.' They looked at me, an unspoken question there clearly for me to see: 'Do you know something we don't know?'

That wasn't the most comfortable time to be Irish in London. I reacted by becoming more Irish than ever before. I would not deny my Irish heritage and vowed to spend more time with my own people. I had even changed my English passport for an Irish one when it was due for renewal, spurred on by Margaret Thatcher making noises about declaring the Irish aliens, with the attendant stigma that would bring.

Tonight I was restless, flicking between television channels, bored with my book. It was a beautiful summer's evening, why shouldn't I go out? I would run myself a bath, get changed and head over to The Galtymore. If there wasn't too much happening I would come home. At least I wouldn't be sitting in on a Saturday night. I put on some black trousers and a short-sleeved pink top; it was always hot inside even in winter, so I knew tonight it would be almost unbearable. My shoes were quite high, but comfortable enough for dancing. I put a few pounds in my purse together with tissues and lipstick and then I was all set. I glanced at the clock, 11.30 p.m., any sensible person would be going to bed now, but not me, it was Saturday night after all.

I paid my money at the door and pushed my way through the sea of people blocking the entrance. It was packed tonight, Big Tom and the Mainliners were playing. They were topping the charts in Ireland, so they always drew a big crowd. I checked my bag in and put the cloakroom ticket in my pocket. The evening was about dancing, I didn't need any encumbrances. I had no sooner got close to the dance floor than the music stopped. In true Irish fashion the girls were standing around the edge of the dance floor. As the music started the men would walk past and ask them to dance; it was like a cattle market, alien to every feminist bone in my body, but I enjoyed it for what it was. I just wanted to dance. A tall blonde-haired man asked me to dance. He looked pleasant and besides it was going to be a set of fast dances so I had nothing to lose. He was a good dancer but didn't attempt to make any conversation so I was happy to make a getaway after the three dances were over.

I danced with many different men that night and was just about to head home as my last partner had turned out to be shorter than me (an unforgivable offence) and spent the whole time shovelling polo mints into his mouth. He was determined to keep dancing with me. I have to make a break for it, I thought, I've had enough. As I was on my way to the cloakroom someone tapped me on the arm, 'Would you like to dance?' I turned round, irritated, I just wanted to go home. My gaze settled on a tall man with twinkling blue eyes and light curly hair.

'Please dance with me,' he said. I relented, he had asked so nicely and I was attracted to his bright, laughing face. How could I resist?

It was good to dance with someone who had plenty to talk about. He told me his name was John, John Monaghan, he was from Donegal, close to the border with Northern Ireland, was working in construction and lived in Willesden, just a few miles away. He danced well and was dressed smartly. Not for him the current Irish male uniform of black trousers with a red jersey. He wore sandy coloured trousers and a blue shirt. His shoes looked smart, well-polished brogues. My mother had always said you could judge a person by the condition of their shoes. I had taken her advice to heart and he definitely passed muster.

I wondered about his age, he had a very boyish look about him and I had a nagging suspicion that he could be younger than me. I was now the grand old age of twenty-three. Surely he wasn't that much younger? Just my luck to meet someone I liked who was too young for me.

All too soon the band played the last song. It was time to go. Everyone stood for the Irish national anthem, a tradition taken very seriously, even in the heart of London.

'Can I walk you home?' he asked.

I argued that I literally lived just across the road, but he insisted. I enjoyed his company so was happy to accept.

'Would you like to come in for coffee?' I asked as we reached the front door.

'That would be great,' he replied.

I showed him into the lounge and he sat down in one of the floral armchairs. I rented a furnished flat so everything was to the taste of the elderly couple that owned it. I handed him the coffee and sat down in the chair opposite him. 'What do you think of the Olympics?' I asked.

We spent the next hour arguing vehemently over the merits of holding the Olympics in Russia; we eventually agreed to disagree, as we couldn't find any common ground. It had been heated but fun to have political discussions at three in the morning. I found John interesting and attractive.

Inevitably the time came for him to leave, it was really late – or early – depending on which way you looked at it. I walked him to the door; he leaned over and kissed me lightly on the lips.

'Would you like to go out next Saturday?'

'That would be great.'

'Ok, I'll come and collect you.'

Off he went.

I sat down on the armchair, smiling to myself, I liked this man. He was intelligent and challenging. It would be good to see him again but he hadn't made a note of my address or phone number. I probably wouldn't ever see him again.

I pushed that depressing thought out of my mind and prepared for bed. I was only going to get a few hours sleep before I needed to head off to work.

Courtship

Next Saturday evening came. I was convinced that John wasn't going to come. Half-heartedly, I got ready to go out, just in case he surprised me, putting on a brown and beige dress, really not my favourite, but in a perverse way not wanting to pull out all the stops in case I was disappointed. I wasn't going to go to a lot of trouble and sit waiting for someone who wasn't going to come.

I settled down in my armchair, put the television on and prepared to wait, I couldn't really take in what has happening on the TV screen as my eyes repeatedly moved to the clock on the mantelpiece. The news finished, now what was I going to watch?

Finally, the doorbell rang. It was him and here I was in this dreadful dress.

'I wasn't sure you'd know where to come,' I said to him as I opened the door, 'I wasn't sure if I'd see you again.'

'I said I'd come and here I am. I always keep my promises.' So we set off for our second evening at The Galtymore. And that was how it all started between John and me.

The next afternoon I gazed out of the bus window as I travelled back from work. I loved to sit upstairs on the Number 16 double-decker bus as it travelled from Victoria station to Cricklewood, passing along Park Lane, Baker Street, Kilburn High Road and then, finally, on to Cricklewood Broadway. I flexed my aching feet in my Gucci shoes. It was hard work, standing all day in the restaurant in the stifling closeness of the London summer. Our uniforms, designed by Gucci, were more classy than practical and I couldn't wait to get out of my fitted dress and into something loose and comfortable. I was partly to blame, too, for feeling so constricted in my dress; the constant temptation of the Godiva chocolates for sale in the open cabinets near the cash register often proved to be too much for me. I really must slow down, I thought to myself, otherwise I will become fat as a fiddle.

My mind drifted to John, I had met him twice now, once at The Galtymore when we had first danced together and then again last night. There was something about him I responded to, he was bright and funny. I felt so attracted to him, I just hoped he felt the same as I did. I smiled to myself as I remembered the fun and laughter of the previous night. I liked him and hoped it would be the start of many more outings together. I stared happily out of the window, the sight of the Cricklewood Post Office sailing by, bringing me back to reality. I'd missed my stop. I gathered my parcels and almost fell down the stairs to get out about half a mile away. That will teach you to daydream, I thought to myself as I set off down the road to my flat.

Just as I put my key in the lock, the phone started to ring. I fumbled to open the door, drop my parcels and just reached the phone in time to hear John's voice. 'Hello, I thought you might be in by now. Do you want to go for a drink later? Or are you too tired?'

What a question, there was no way I would miss this. I tried to sound nonchalant: 'Of course I'm not too tired, a drink would be great.'

'Ok, I'll be there at eight.'

'See you then.'

I hurried to pack away my shopping and then lay down on the bed. Things were working out well, he seemed quite keen. I looked at the clock; I could snatch an hour's sleep and still have time to shower, change and be ready by eight o'clock. I started thinking about what to wear.

John arrived promptly at eight.

'I thought we could go to The Tara Club,' he said. 'It's just down the road from where I live and maybe we'll bump into some friends of mine.'

We took a cab through to the club and, as he had predicted, he managed to pick out some of his friends among the hordes of young Irish who flocked there on a Sunday night. It was noisy and smoky, with a band playing in the corner. Not the greatest place to carry on a conversation but enjoyable none the less.

'There's Elizabeth,' he said, pointing to an older blonde woman in jeans and a denim jacket, surrounded by a group of friends.

'Who's Elizabeth?' I asked.

'My aunt.'

She looks far trendier than any of my aunts, I thought to myself as he took me by the hand and led me over to meet her.

'Hello, me darling,' she said to John, hugging him tightly.

'You must be Mary,' she said to me, 'I've heard a lot about you.'

She had a pleasant, relaxed way about her and I found her easy to talk to. The one thing I found strange was that she didn't have an Irish accent and sounded like a Londoner. I asked her why this was.

'My father, John's grandfather, came over to London to work,' she said. 'So we kids were brought up here, John's mother, Margaret, too, and our brothers John and PJ. We all stayed in London except Margaret who went back to Ireland, so it's like two different sides of the family. An Irish side and a London Irish side.'

John had described his mother as a solid Irish farmer's wife, very different from the blonde, vibrant woman that was her sister.

Elizabeth chatted happily to John and me for an hour or so before going off to rejoin her friends. That wasn't so bad, I thought to myself. My first encounter with John's family, it went off quite well. I suppose I should introduce him to Kathryn now that it seems to be getting quite serious.

There was just the niggling doubt about his age. He looked young, but how young was he? I decided to broach the subject when we got back to my flat later that evening. Easier said than done, how could I bring it up in conversation? On top of that I had to tell him I was going to Ireland for a few weeks, a trip that had been planned a long time ago.

'I've got a trip to Ireland planned next month,' I told him. 'It was arranged ages ago, I'll be away for about two weeks.'

'I'll miss you,' he replied.

'It's just two weeks, it will go quickly. I've promised my aunt Annie, so I can't change my plans.'

'I know,' he said, 'we'll just have to spend lots of time together before then.'

I wanted to talk about his age but couldn't find an easy way to do it. The longer I waited, the harder it became to bring it up. I'll find out soon enough, I thought to myself. We are getting on so well, what's the big deal anyway?

We arranged to meet the night before I was due to leave. We were going for dinner in Cricklewood. I dressed carefully, putting on my favourite brown dress that I knew John really liked. We had a great evening, talking so much that the waiter battled to get us to choose from the menu. We walked back to the flat holding hands.

As I busied myself in the kitchen, John came up behind me, circling my waist with his hands and nuzzling into my neck. 'There's something I need to tell you,' he said.

'What's that?' I asked.

'You must have been wondering about my age. From some of the things I've told you, you must have realised I am younger than you. I know you are twenty-three, but I am only seventeen, does that matter?'

'Not at all,' I replied, relieved that it was out in the open. My instincts had been right. He was younger than me, seventeen, but a very mature and independent one at that. 'It makes no difference to me whatsoever,' I said as I turned to kiss him.

'You're very kind,' he said, fumbling in his jacket pocket. 'I have something for you.'

He took a small box out of his pocket and handed it to me.

I ripped off the wrapping paper and opened the box to find a beautiful gold cross and chain.

'Please wear it while you are away,' he said.

I hugged and kissed him. 'I love it, and I'll wear it always, thank you so much.'

Could it get any better? I wasn't sure. All I knew was that I was mad about John. So he was younger than me, but what difference did that make? We got on so well together, loved to dance, go to restaurants, listen to music, it was just perfect.

I vowed to tell my family all about him when I saw them. Then I would arrange for them to meet him. I knew he was going to become a special part of my life.

'He sounds nice,' my mother said to me, 'you should bring him to Cambridge for the day one Sunday, and then your father and I can meet him.' I had told them John was younger than me but hadn't quite had the courage to tell them just how much younger, that was irrelevant anyway. My mother was three years older than my father so what was the big deal?

Kathryn agreed to meet us for a drink the following week. Before going to meet her I had gone with John to his grandmother's house in Willesden. I knew he was close to her, closer probably than to his mother. He often spoke of Granny with great love and affection, whereas he hardly mentioned his mother. His grandmother had a broad Irish accent; she was short, with curly, sandy-coloured hair. She shook my hand warmly.

'John tells me you are a great girl,' she said as she offered me a cup of coffee. We spoke easily for an hour or so while John discreetly busied himself in the garden with his grandfather.

'She likes you, I can tell,' he said to me as we got into the car. 'She's very straightforward; she would have shown it if she didn't.'

I grinned back at him; it was our day for meeting the family. I was sure Kathryn would be fine too. I knew she would report back to our parents but I didn't care. John and I were getting on well and I knew she would be happy for me. I was right.

'He's nice,' she said to me the day after the three of us met at The Castle in Child's Hill for drinks. 'He's so caring and attentive. You can see he's a bit younger than you, but it's not a big deal.'

'Will you come to Paris with me for the weekend?' John asked a few weeks later.

I nodded eagerly, 'Of course I will.'

'I thought we could go in a couple of week's time, take the hover-craft and explore the sights.'

I smiled to myself, now here was a man after my own heart, I so loved to travel and go away to places on impulse. John had told me he had not had the same opportunities to travel as I had, never venturing outside Ireland apart from visiting London, but he was eager to explore new things.

We made plans for our trip. We would do all the standard tourist things but also intended to explore some out of the way places on our own. We visited the Eiffel Tower, Notre Dame and spent a balmy summer's evening on the steps of the Sacre Coeur, listening to students playing folk music while young people from many different countries sang along. We held hands as we wandered the narrow streets of the Left Bank, looking for an intimate restaurant to eat dinner. We settled on one a little off the tourist track and toasted our trip with champagne and *moules frites*.

It was in Paris that I realised that I had fallen in love with John; we shared a passion for life. I loved his sense of fun and adventure and the way he always made me feel so special. He was very much a man's man, enjoying drinks at the Irish Club with his friends, telling jokes and stories, but he also had a gentle, sensitive side, making me feel cherished and protected with little gestures, impromptu presents and flowers. I thought back to the gift he had given me a few weeks previously:

'I brought you something back from Ireland,' John said to me as he handed me a small parcel. 'When I saw it I just had to get it for you, I knew you would like it.'

I hugged him tightly and reached for my present. He had only been away for a week but I missed him so much. He had gone over to Ireland for a wedding; one of his colleagues in London had gone home to get married. John was going more from a sense of duty than anything else. I hadn't been able to take time off from work, having been to Ireland earlier, so I couldn't go with him. It was the longest time we had been apart since we had started going out six months previously. John was such a part of my life now; it seemed strange not to have him close by. We met often during the week, even if it was just for a quick drink and, of course, we spent all of our weekends together.

I was never the most polite of people when it came to opening presents. Ripping off the paper, I found a stone-cast Celtic mythical figure, shaped like a flattened griffin. I read the description on the back: 'Cong Love Token from County Mayo'. I smiled; Cong was just a few miles away from Ballinrobe.

The description continued:

It is a symbol of love, always watching, ever giving. Whoever carries it has a a a promise of love in their arms.

Not of 'I love you because I need you but of I need you because I love you'.

'It's beautiful, thank you,' I said as I kissed John. 'I will keep it with me always so that your love will always be with me.' I couldn't have been happier. I felt so secure in John's love and just knew that this token would be with me wherever I went and would always be a reminder of how I was loved.

I adored the way he didn't ignore me when we went out in a crowd with other couples. So many of the other women complained that their Irish partners ignored them for the entire evening, but that was not the case with John. He would regularly check that I was all right, coming over to give me a hug and whisper in my ear as I sat with the other women. My friends often said they wished their boyfriends were more like John, showing consideration and treating them as equals. It was still unfortunately a fact of life that Irish men generally subscribed to macho principles, expecting their women to socialise among themselves and not interfere with their male bonding when they went out together. I was so lucky that John broke the mould.

Our life in London grew into a pattern of socialising together and with our friends. We made it a point to go away regularly for weekends to Devon, Cornwall, Sussex, always happy in each other's company, John surprising me constantly with presents. Things were just perfect, we were so happy together and it showed. Our friends called us 'the happy couple', asking us what our secret was. We had no idea; we just knew what we had was precious and we were determined to nurture it.

 # *Wedding*

'We need to talk,' John said, after we had been out to The Tara Club and had a raucous time with friends one August evening. It was 2 a.m. and all I could think about was climbing into bed. I had to be up at 8 a.m. for work the next day so I couldn't afford to miss any more sleep. But John looked determined; he was an easy-going person until he had an idea in his head and then he became totally single-minded. I could see this was one of those occasions.

'I'll make some coffee,' I called out as I went into the kitchen, something telling me that this wasn't going to be a quick discussion. I took out the jar of biscuits, John had a sweet tooth and I made sure I always had plenty in stock. Tonight I had chocolate-chip cookies; he loved those, as well as the Irish biscuits you could buy in Cricklewood, like Kimberley and Mikado. I carried the tray into the lounge and sat down next to him. He had already put some music on. Rod Stewart played softly in the background.

We had been going out for just over a year now, visiting Devon to celebrate our first anniversary. We spent most of our free time together, the future looked good.

I settled down next to him. I loved to cuddle and would snuggle up at the slightest opportunity, we spent many hours cuddling. Tonight he pulled away, a serious look on his face, 'I am going to South Africa to work.'

I looked at him, unable to believe what I was hearing. A bald statement of fact, no prior warning or discussion, he had made up his mind. Where was I in this equation?

'There are lots of opportunities there,' he continued, 'I know I can make a go of it. I'm doing all right here but if I go to South Africa and work hard, I know I will make my fortune.' He had always been ambitious and single-minded about making money.

'What about me?' I stammered. 'Did you think about me?'

'You can come and join me.'

My shock and hurt turned to anger at his assumption. There were so many reasons why it was not that easy. I was close to my family and didn't want to move too far away from them. In addition, I had a moral objection to living in South Africa. As a student in London in the late seventies, I was aware of the injustices being committed by the system of apartheid, I couldn't contemplate living there and accepting the status quo. Even now, in 1980, things hadn't changed for the better.

I felt betrayed and angry. How could he just assume I would meekly follow wherever he went? I pulled away from him and moved to another armchair. Who was this man opposite me and how well did I really know him?

He glanced at me, surprised at my outburst. I was usually so calm and accepting, he had never seen me react so strongly to anything before. 'I'm not going to change my mind. I need to do this. I'll phone you tomorrow, we'll talk some more.'

I nodded briefly, not wanting to grace him with a reply and glared at the empty room as he gathered up his things and let himself out. The wind had completely gone out of my sails. Why had I not seen this coming? Why wasn't I an equal partner in this relationship? Who did he think he was?

I knew it was useless trying to sleep now, so I poured myself some more coffee and tried to understand what had just happened and come to terms with it. John had been unsettled since his run in with the police a few months previously; it had been a bad experience for both of us.

I was woken in the early hours of a Monday morning by the sound of the doorbell. I glanced at the clock: 3.30 a.m. I had only been in bed for just over an hour. John and I had been out for a late supper and he had left for home at about 2 a.m. I put on my dressing gown and went to the door, I opened it slowly, making sure the security chain was on. A tall policeman held up his badge for inspection.

'Do you know a Michael Monaghan?' he asked, in a broad Scottish accent.

'Yes, I do,' I replied, quickly remembering that John's identification was that of his brother Michael as he had been using Michael's driver's licence.

'Can you account for his whereabouts this evening?'

I confirmed that we had been to The American Steakhouse on Cricklewood Broadway for our weekly ritual of steak, followed by strawberry tart.

'What time did you leave?'

'11 o'clock.'

'And then where did you go?'

'It was a beautiful evening so we went for a walk in the park, we got back here at about 12.30.'

'Did anyone see you?'

'No.'

'So no-one else can confirm your story?'

'No. What is this about?'

'There has been an assault on the owner of the minicab office around the corner. We picked up Michael Monaghan close to there. The owner confirmed that the thug was Irish and positively identified Michael.'

'That's nonsense,' I replied. 'He has been with me the entire evening.'

'Thank you for your time,' he replied, walking back out into the street.

I got back into bed but couldn't sleep. It was true; John didn't have much of an alibi, just me. No one else had seen him; I hoped it would be enough.

He phoned me later that morning. 'Thanks for confirming what I told them. Just as well you remembered I had Michael's licence on me. They pounced on me as I was walking down the road and dragged me into the office to be identified. They roughed me up quite badly, you know how they love us Irish these days.'

I found out later the police had interviewed my landlord to get a bit more background on John; coming as he did from Donegal, near the border with the North of Ireland, increased their suspicions of him. It was not a good time to be a young Irishman in London. I could understand John's need to leave England, but still wished he had at least discussed his plans with me before presenting me with a *fait accompli.*

He left London a month later, in September 1980, with no job waiting for him. He had decided to enter South Africa on a return ticket and take his chances. My friend Lindsay who worked with me at the restaurant had a friend, Dottie, who lived in Johannesburg. We arranged for John to stay with her until he found his feet. I was still bitter at what was happening but had come around to accepting the situation. I had no choice anyway; nothing I said would change things.

The plan was for him to go in search of work, settle in, get his work permit and then I would consider going over. I was very firm about the fact that the best I would do was visit, not stay. I needed to take a look and then decide for myself.

It was a tearful farewell as he set off with just one suitcase to seek his fortune. I knew I would miss him terribly but I vowed to keep myself busy and carry on with my life. I had no intention of moping around.

His letters came regularly as he wrote at least two or three times a week. It was too expensive to phone. I was secure in his love as he wrote of his longing for us to be together, and his sorrow at leaving me:

You know I was looking at the photos one night I was lonely and I saw in your eyes what you were going through when you were having the photos taken. I'm sorry for putting you through all this Mary, it's not nice at all but I tell you one thing, I will make it up to you one way or another and a hundred times over.

...

I can't think of anyone else I would like to spend the rest of my life with. I love you and I want you by my side all the time.

...

I miss your loving and your caring. I am very empty inside, I am very alone and lonely, I want my woman. But I went away and made her very sad and I'm very sorry. I made a mistake leaving her and now I want to make up for it. I will keep giving you all I can. Mary we have a life ahead together and a lot of happy times together.

...

We have another thing to look forward to. A whole life. I will try my best to give you a good life and to love you always. I can't wait to make love to you again.

He had got a job with a Scotsman, Mike Kelly, who ran a firm called Kelly Industrial Painters and was sent to work on a contract, on the mines in the Free State, a hot, dusty, barren area of the country. He was working hard, making good money and soon started to nag me about visiting.

I was stubborn; it wasn't as simple as that. I had a job and a flat at a good rent; it would be hard to get as good a deal again. I didn't want to give everything up. I agreed to go over in January for three months, giving up my job but keeping my flat in case I wanted to come back to London. It meant I could still spend Christmas with my family and also do my two-week stint at the Miss World beauty contest. I had worked there for the last three years as an interpreter/chaperone, looking after six South American contestants. It was hard work but fun and I didn't want to miss it. I had the advantage of doing everything the contestants did in terms of seeing shows, and attending gala dinners, without having to parade in front of millions of people. It was always a great two weeks. I felt a bit like a celebrity myself, staying in de luxe hotels, hobnobbing with the rich and famous.

That year, the week before the contest was spent in Miami, the first time I had visited the States. It was great to be busy as I was missing John terribly. I was running late for a chaperone's meeting when the phone rang in my hotel room. It was John; he'd managed to trace the hotel number. He sounded tired and lonely, with no one there to talk to.

'I just needed to hear your voice,' he said. 'It's so difficult here on my own. I'm working long hours, staying in a real dump of a hotel in the middle of the Free State. All I seem to do is work and sleep. How are things there? I miss you so much; it's not the same being here without you.'

'I know but we agreed, you would settle in first then I would come over in January.'

'It just seems so far away.'

'I know, we'll just have to hang in there.'

'I want you to marry me,' he said. 'Will you marry me?'

'Are you down on your knees?'

'Hold on a second – I am now.'

'Ok, propose to me again.'

'Please Mary, marry me?'

'Of course I will.'

'That's decided then.'

We laughed at how easy it was to make the decision and agreed to talk again when I was back home.

I looked at my watch, I was desperately late, and I ran into the meeting room to be greeted by stony faces, irritated at being kept waiting. I couldn't keep my secret. 'John's just proposed!' I blurted out.

A week later a card arrived for me in the post, my address was on it but John had addressed it to 'Mrs Monaghan'. The card said, 'Thank you for making me so happy.'

The letters just kept on coming:

You know it will be so nice when we get married I promise you I will do all I can to make you happy. It will be just you and me against the world, side by side, all the way. We will be 'the happy couple' once again.

...

I'm very sorry that I couldn't be with you for Christmas but I promise you that we will have many more Christmases together, Mary I love you very much and I want to marry you and I want us to live happily together until we get old. I don't want to spend any more time without you. I knew I would miss you when I left but it was as though I left a part of me behind. A big part of me was left with that little woman of mine. A very special Mary who I know loves me, I'm so sorry for making her so sad but I will try to make up for it. I love you so much and I want you and I miss you. But soon I will have you with me, then

I can start living again. I will have something to live for.

...

Hello my little wife, it's your husband taking up the pen again. You know the one that's in Africa that loves you so much. Boy it isn't long now. Only three weeks and I'll have my baby back in my arms again. That will be a day to remember won't it? Can you believe it is 4 months? It's a long time but only very short compared to the long and happy life we are going to have ahead of us, just you and me against the world. That's the way we like it. You see I still love you very much. O my darling I can't wait to have you back again. I know the mistake I made leaving you, I should have hauled you with me. I know we must take it slowly in the beginning because it has been such a long time and it will take a bit of getting used to. But we will try hard and I know it will work out just fine. We will have lots of good times and go plenty of places. Love you very much, my 'wife to be'.

January arrived and I set off for South Africa, apprehensive at what would await me. John had told me he spent weeks working away at times but he would make sure he was around town for my first few weeks.

My parents were outwardly supportive of my plans, but I knew that deep down both they and Kathryn had reservations. They were worried about the age difference between us and also our diverse backgrounds. I had had the benefit of a university education and had travelled the world and John had had the benefit of none of that, leaving school as he had at the age of seventeen. They were worried we would not be able to relate on an intellectual level. I would hear none of it. I was convinced John was the man for me. I was giving everything up for a future in South Africa with no guarantees.

I slept fitfully on the plane, too hyped up to fall into a deep sleep. I had brought a dress to change into, as I wanted to make an impression when I first arrived. It was a totally impractical cream silk dress; easily creased and it made me look like a ghost when I put it on next to my pale skin. Of course, at the time, I thought it looked very chic and that was all that mattered. John said later he didn't care how I looked when I arrived, just as long as I was there with him.

I scanned the sea of faces in the arrivals hall as I moved through from customs. What if he wasn't there? But there he was, his face tanned and his hair a lot longer than I had ever seen it. He still had the same broad grin as he gripped me in a hug so tight it took my breath away. We grinned at each other, hardly able to believe that we were reunited. We tried to hold hands as we pushed the trolley to the car park, but ended up veering in so many directions that we gave up.

He led me to a beige panel van with 'Kelly Industrial Painters' emblazoned on the side. 'I've put some plastic on the front seat; I didn't want to mess up your clothes, as the seats can get a bit grubby.' I smiled thankfully; the van was in stark contrast to my smart outfit. I climbed up into the passenger seat, smoothing down my dress. We hugged and kissed some more before setting off.

'I've found us a flat in Hillbrow; they're quite hard to come by. It's not got too much furniture as I thought you might like to look for things, you have such a good eye for decorating.'

I stared out of the window. So this was Africa, so hot and bright, but there was a vibrancy about it that appealed to me. I liked what I saw.

It took longer than I had anticipated to find a job, but furnishing and decorating the flat occupied most of my time. After the first week John was at work and I tried hard to keep myself busy. I scoured the paper daily for jobs and eventually after many interviews I got one, working in a book agency. It was a small family business run by an elderly Jewish couple that took me under their wing.

Now that I had decided to stay, there was the additional stress over whether I would or wouldn't get a work permit. Eventually, after several visits to the Department of Home Affairs, I was granted one. John wasn't so lucky, as he didn't have any qualifications and it took several years before he was able to get residence. This was further complicated by the fact that he didn't want to be called up for the SA Defence Force, a distinct possibility as he fell within the eligible age group. The last thing he wanted was to be called up for military duty. It would interfere with his plans to make his fortune; that had become his sole purpose in life.

He worked hard, often on contracts around the country. I was happy enough to have time to myself as I had always been used to my independence. I made friends easily and wasn't afraid to be on my own. A year after starting work at the book agency I got my permanent residence status and was then free to look for any job I wanted. I was no longer tied down. I needed more stimulation and applied for a job as Supervisor of Customer Services at American Express Card.

I started work at American Express in 1983 and spent eleven years there. It was there I made many good friends who saw me through the ups and downs of life. It was hard work dealing with customer complaints and at that stage there were a lot of those. The Customer Service department was in disarray. I knew what I had taken on when I came back from lunch on my first day to be greeted by smiles of approval and comments about the last two new recruits having gone to lunch never to return.

Life took on a certain routine, we were young and independent, and John and I both worked hard and played hard. We had no family in South Africa and led a relatively selfish existence, doing whatever we wanted. We enjoyed the good life, eating out in fine restaurants, spending weekends away. We made a lot of Irish friends and used to meet over the weekend at the Irish Club in Hillbrow. I went back to England periodically to visit my parents in Cambridge and Kathryn in London, trying to catch up with them every year. John had no desire to visit his family. It seemed that when he left them at seventeen to go to England he had cut himself off from them totally.

I found it hard to understand his coldness to his family, it was so different to the close-knit family ties that I had. Both Kathryn and I had left home at eighteen to go to college and university but we still retained at least weekly contact with our parents, keeping in touch with them as important things happened in our lives. No major event would go by without our sharing it with our parents. We had a stable loving family relationship in stark contrast to the cold and remote one John had with his family.

He was one of five children brought up on a farm in County Donegal, in the North West of Ireland. He didn't finish his last year at school, deciding to disappear to England to work after an altercation with his mother. I never did get to the bottom of the issue surrounding it. All I knew was that he didn't make contact with his family for many years afterwards and really only responded to their contact with him, never initiating it himself. I got the impression that there was an extreme coldness there, but I wasn't allowed to get close enough to understand why. He didn't like to talk about his parents, or his life at home in Ireland, saying that this was no longer a part of his life. They had never done anything for him so why must he worry about them. I tried to encourage him to write to his parents but he just wasn't interested, so it was left up to me to send them Christmas cards and the odd letter.

'I think we should get married soon,' John said to me one winter's evening when we were snuggled up on the sofa.

We had talked about marriage on and off over the three years that I had been in South Africa, but somehow we never seemed to find the right time to do it. I was still keenly aware that I was six years older than John. I was twenty-seven and he was then only twenty-one so I didn't feel it was a good idea to rush into anything. I had experienced many things that John hadn't. I knew what I wanted but I needed to be sure that he was equally certain, being acutely aware that he had only been seventeen when I had met him and that he had spent all his adult years with me, never having had another relationship or having experienced life outside what we had experienced together.

'We'll have to invite quite a few of my business acquaintances,' he said.

I kicked against the idea. I had always maintained that I wanted a small wedding. I wanted it to be meaningful and I didn't want to be caught up in all the irrelevant side issues that ended up dominating and overwhelming the true purpose of the day.

'So many people will be disappointed if we don't invite them,' he said.

It wasn't what I wanted but I gave in. I could see it was important to him. He wanted a big, splashy affair, he loved to entertain lavishly.

'As long as I can organise it in a day. I'm not spending my time on trivial things.'

He nodded his head in agreement.

I drove to work in town the next day from our rented house in Mondeor, to the south of Johannesburg, there was frost in the fields on the side of the highway, it was mid winter. Roll on summer I thought. We had set the date, 14th December 1985; it would be a popular one as it heralded the start of the builder's holidays. I walked into Pam's office clutching a steaming hot cup of coffee. Pam was my boss, but also a close friend.

'We've set a date,' I said.

'Are you engaged?'

'No, it seems a bit pointless after living together for so long.'

'When are you getting married?'

'On the 14th of December.'

'That doesn't give you long to arrange it.'

'I know; only four months, that's why I want to spend the morning on the phone arranging everything. I must sort it out today.'

She looked at me in astonishment.

'I'm serious,' I said. 'I don't want this to take over my life. There are just some important things to worry about, the church, the priest, a venue for the reception and a live band. I'm not worried about anything else.'

'What about the photographer?'

'I'm not planning on using one. When I'm a guest I hate wasting an hour of my time at weddings while the bride and groom pose for the perfect photo.'

'And bridesmaids?'

'I'm not having any.'

I was determined that if I had to have a big wedding I was going to do it my way.

'I'm posting the invitations,' I said to John, 'do you want to write anything on the one for your parents?'

'Don't send it yet,' he said. 'Wait until closer to the time. I want them to know it's happening, but I don't want them to come.'

I couldn't believe that he felt like that, but he was stubborn and had no intention of changing his mind. I knew better than to try to argue with him.

My mother and Kathryn knew about the wedding already, I had phoned them as soon as we had set the date. Mother was so excited and couldn't wait to visit, she had been very lonely since my father had died the previous year. Kathryn on the other hand was not impressed that we were getting married in South Africa and couldn't get off school in time to make it over. So the only family either of us had at our wedding was my mother.

It was a great day; full of love and laughter, the service was simple but meaningful. We held the reception at Jameson's Restaurant in town. We hadn't stinted on food and drink and had a great party, dancing to the sound of The Beer Mugs, an Irish band. It was a happy, carefree day, unmarred by any degree of formality.

We settled easily into married life, nothing really had changed. We had moved into our own house in Mondeor. John's business was going well. We didn't have a care in the world.

Birthday wishes

That was ten years ago and it was now two months since John left for Australia.

As agreed, he had made no contact with me for the full eight weeks. I tried to keep myself busy, working long hours but the nights and weekends seemed, oh, so long and empty. As the bills continued to come in, I started to realise the full extent of John's financial hassles. Our situation was dire; just as well we had agreed to put the house on the market, I thought, as it would give us some much-needed cash. Every day I was receiving calls from John's suppliers, requesting payment, but there was no money in our bank account and I knew I had no way of paying them. The amounts were huge and even with the sale of our house I knew I wouldn't have enough. I hadn't realised the full extent of John's company's debt until now, as phone calls were replaced with summonses arriving weekly at the house. Eventually the sheriff of the court arrived to take away the furniture and contents of John's office in the house. Everything was falling apart. I didn't know what to do. I was glad that he would be back in a month or so; he would help share the burden and come up with a plan.

Nigel was faithful to his charge to look after me through all this. He and I had started scouting around for another house, a run-down property in a less affluent suburb for John to renovate on his return. All we would need was a small deposit and we would be able to afford the repayments. I missed John so much and was starting to regret my agreement to have no contact for three months, but I had made the commitment and had to take the consequences. I kept telling myself that the time left until his return, just over a month now, would go quickly.

It was my birthday on the 22nd April, not too long until John would be back, I thought. The months since he had been gone had been difficult ones and despite my vow to be strong the strain was taking its toll. John had always made such a fuss of my birthday and now he just wasn't here. My friends meant well by asking me to go out, but my heart wasn't in it. Eventually, I accepted Maggie's offer to go to the cinema just to keep everyone happy.

In my heart I had hoped that John might contact me but I remembered our agreement, no contact for three months, and I respected that. It would give him time to get his thoughts straight and prepare for his change of career when he returned. I knew he would have taken the failure of his company very hard. He would feel that he had lost face in the Irish community, as he had always been a success story. Nobody knew the extent of his financial problems; he liked to put a show of affluence on for others even when times were tough. His pride was injured now and I knew he would find it hard to face his friends again and admit failure.

My phone hadn't stopped ringing all day, all my friends were anxious to check that I was doing all right and although I really appreciated their concern I could feel the unanswered question hanging in the air. They so wanted to ask – have you heard from John? But they knew better than to broach the subject. By the time Maggie and I left for the cinema there was no one left to phone me except John and I resigned myself to the fact that he wouldn't. I knew he was travelling around Australia; I was able to monitor his progress by the credit card charges that were coming through. He was spending quite freely in restaurants and bars and although I was relieved to be able to get some idea of his whereabouts, I was starting to panic at the rising bills to be paid, and was irritated at the extravagant charges he was billing to his card. So much for living frugally, I said to myself as yet another Diner's bill came in.

After the film it was late and I was tired. I declined Maggie's suggestion of a quick coffee before heading home to bed. I parked the car in the driveway and took the present she had given me out of the boot. It was a beautiful candle. 'Use it in your bathroom,' she said. She knew how I loved to have scented candlelit baths. Maybe, I thought, I should have one tonight, it might calm me a bit.

The front door was sticking as usual. If I was going to sell the house I would have to do something about it, not the best first impression for a prospective buyer. Finally the door gave way. I tumbled into the hallway to be greeted by the message light on my answering machine blinking. Two messages. Could it be John? Surely not? I couldn't work out what the time difference was. I pressed play, dissolving into tears as I heard the sound of his voice. I couldn't believe I had missed his call; his voice filled the room as I played the message over and over.

'Hello, Mr Monaghan, you're not going to be able to get through here.'

'I know, thank you very much. I'll try again later.' Beep ...

'Hello sweetheart, Happy Birthday, I'll phone again later, Happy Birthday.'

Hearing his voice made me realise just how much I missed him. Now I had to wait for him to phone again. I just hoped he would manage to get through later.

I slept fitfully that night, expecting the phone to ring at any minute. At 4 a.m. it rang and I heard an Australian voice on the other end.

'Is that Mary Monaghan?'

'Yes it is.'

'Will you accept a reverse charge call from John Monaghan?'

There was no question that I would.

'Hello sweetheart. Happy Birthday.'

I burst into tears, the loneliness of the last months overwhelming me.

'Hello. How are you?'

We spoke non-stop. John telling me how tough it had been for him, living on a shoestring, working here and there, travelling around, sometimes only surviving on potatoes and cabbage. It was so good to speak to him; all my worries seemed to fade away and I completely forgot to ask about all the restaurant charges billed to his Diners card. It was just so great to hear his voice.

'We've had a wedding invitation; Patricia is getting married in Ireland.'

'When is it?'

'In two weeks time.'

'What do you want me to do? Do you want me to come back for it?'

'It's up to you. Whatever you want.'

'Do you want to go?'

'I'm relaxed either way. I know it would mean your coming back here early and then going over to Ireland.'

'I'm not too bothered about the wedding but I'll come back if you really want me to.'

'No, don't worry, it would be expensive, we would have to fly to Ireland for it.'

It was really out of the question in our financial situation. I was so tempted to ask him to come back, Patricia was his sister and of all his family members the only one he was close to, but we had agreed on three months and I wanted to stick to this. Besides what difference would a couple of weeks make?

He asked me how things were going with the sale of our house in Mondeor. I had had a few people come in and look, but nothing definite had come up yet. I had been looking for somewhere to buy. I told him how I had seen a place in Regent's Park, a run-down suburb in the south of Johannesburg. It was in a state, rotting window frames and doors, peeling wallpaper but it had potential. The first thing it needed was a good coat of paint. Nigel had looked at it with me. At least it was better than some of the places we had seen in Krugersdorp West. They had given a new meaning to the word hovel, broken windows, doors hanging off hinges, no inside toilets, derelict and filthy. My heart sank when I thought of living there.

Regent's Park was not much better. The houses looked neglected, not from lack of pride just from lack of funds. It was a far cry from our beautiful house in Mondeor with its pool and guest cottages. This place just looked so shabby and depressing. I gritted my teeth, I would just have to live with it in the meantime, I was sure it would all work out in the end.

'If we do decide to put in an offer, should we paint it and fix it up a bit before you come back?'

'No. Please don't. I don't want anyone but me to work on it.'

'You'll be here in no time anyway, so what's a few weeks' delay?'

We continued to talk about this and that, but knowing that the call was expensive we had to wrap up the conversation quickly.

'It won't be long,' John said. 'I love you sweetheart. Happy Birthday again.'

The line went dead. I cried bitterly. I so wanted to ask him to give me a date when he was coming back but I didn't want to force the issue. I didn't want to ask the question, as it would have broken our pact. It was so good to speak to him but there were still so many unanswered questions. So many of his responses were evasive, he hadn't really volunteered very much information about what he had been doing.

When was he coming back? He should be booking his ticket about now. It was good to speak to him but also unsettling. My feeling of unease returned. Why did he not mention his return date? How long would I have to wait for him to come and fix the new house? How would our relationship be after all that had happened?

I knew I wouldn't be able to sleep any more so I got up out of the bed, pulled on my dressing gown and padded through to the kitchen to make myself some coffee. I grabbed the jar from the cupboard, it was almost empty, but had just enough for a few more cups. It was nearly payday so I'd be able to stock up again soon. I sat at the kitchen table my hands cupping the mug, every now and again lifting it to my lips, battling to swallow, my stomach churning as an overwhelming feeling of nausea gripped me. I sensed something wrong, quite what I didn't know. Again the feeling of foreboding came over me. I played the answering machine tape over and over, taking comfort from the sound of his voice.

'Hello sweetheart, Happy Birthday,' John's voice filled the silence of the early morning.

At least he had phoned me. What was wrong with me? Why was I feeling so empty? I should have been glad that I had spoken to him. I kept telling myself to cheer up but it was easier said than done.

As dawn broke, I went into the garden and walked around. Smelling the flowers calmed me and I eventually went back into the house and ran myself a bath. I needed to relax before heading off to work. I took the tape out of the machine and replaced it with another one. I knew I would need to listen to John's voice again before the two weeks were over.

Chicken farming

The three months were well over and there was no sign of John. I had had no contact with him since my birthday in April. Now it was almost June and I'd received not a word. Everything had been worked around the fact that he would return after three months. I had estimated that I would have enough money to manage to pay the bills and just keep my head above water financially until then, but now everything was falling apart. I dreaded my phone ringing to find another one of John's creditors demanding money. I printed out our bank statements and worked out the monthly budget, noting an ever-increasing shortfall. The house in Mondeor had been sold and I would soon have to move to the new house in Regent's Park.

I glanced behind me into the dining room to find Sarah standing there still as a statue. She had been our domestic worker and part of the family since 1985, when we had first moved to our house in Mondeor. She was the wife of Samson, one of John's drivers, a round stocky woman with a great sense of fun and a beaming smile. We had shared many happy moments together and she was a firm favourite with my mother. On Mother's visits to us she had spent long hours in the kitchen over endless cups of tea talking to Sarah. She was a special part of our family and had felt John's departure just as keenly as I did. She knew money was tight and had offered to reduce her hours and work somewhere else as well, so I could reduce my monthly payment to her. As she watched me from the dining room her gaze was steady and unflinching; her face set tightly, there was no sign of her usual infectious smile.

I lay curled up like a ball on the settee crying. I had watched many films in which I had condemned, as overacting, characters howling with anguish and grief, but now I understood them as I hardly recognised as human the sounds coming from my own being: they were those of a wounded, abandoned animal. Finally I had no energy left to cry, I lay whimpering quietly. Turning round slowly, I found Sarah still there, looking at me, saying nothing, her eyes full of tears. She was there for me, she didn't need to say anything, I understood.

I got up from the settee, attempting to smile reassuringly at her. 'Don't worry, it will be all right, go to bed now.'

I walked through to the kitchen to put the kettle on for yet another a cup of coffee, remembering too late that I had run out days ago and had decided it was an unnecessary expense. I'd just have to make do with drinking coffee at the office; buying food was far more important. I drank some water, threw off my clothes and got into bed, curling up, clutching my pillow and falling into an exhausted sleep.

Some time after this the purchase of the new house in Regent's Park came through and the day of the move arrived. The movers came with a rusty blue bakkie, which looked as if it wasn't long for this world. They planned to shuttle my furniture through to the house in five or six trips. It was a clear, sunny day, thankfully, as there was no protection for the furniture from the elements.

I gave them the address and said I would meet them there. They pulled up behind me at the new house, took one look at the overgrown garden, the gate hanging on one hinge, the rotting window frames and the man in charge said to me, 'You can't be moving here, madam? What about your lovely house?'

I brushed bits of twig from my trousers as I walked up the excuse for a driveway and attempted a reassuring smile, 'Yes I am, I have great plans for this place.'

He didn't look convinced, shrugged his shoulders and glanced meaningfully at his co-workers as if to say this woman is really mad.

After a few more trips everything was in place in Regent's Park, with just a settee remaining in Mondeor. I refused to make the final move to the new house until the very last minute, as I had still had no contact with John. The phone in Mondeor was his only means of contacting me, so I resolved to stay at the end of the phone line for as long as possible, bedding down every night with a sleeping bag in the eeriness of the empty house, willing him to phone.

Eventually I had to accept defeat and move to the new house, and become accustomed to my new surroundings. Most of my boxes remained unpacked because I knew I would have to have some work done to fix up the place, the only problem being that I had no money to do anything. I had not received a cent from the sale of the house in Mondeor; John's creditors had attached the proceeds. I had to use my salary to cover everything, the new house, running expenses, food and, of course, the bond for the farm in Boons, just outside Magaliesburg. It was just impossible: I couldn't come out on my salary alone – something had to give.

The farm had been bought after we had been married for four years and was registered in my name to give me some form of financial security, but now instead it became a millstone around my neck. It was an old rambling farmhouse. We had spent many weekends renovating and decorating with Nigel to restore it to its former splendour. It was a tranquil place, set far away from civilisation and it gave me a space in which to reflect and revitalise my flagging spirits. It had no electricity, so we had stayed there using candles and oil lamps, cooking on a wood stove. The pace of life there was slow and it was good for the soul, but finding the money to cover the payments was now a real problem.

I went there most weekends with Pam. We had been friends for years, starting work at American Express at about the same time. She was a survivor and had been through many tough times in her life. I could always count on her to think of ways to get through the bad times. She was great at coming up with money-making schemes and one Saturday afternoon in December 1993, as we sat on the stoep looking at the bluegums in the distance she said, 'Chickens! Why don't you buy chickens? You can sell the eggs and get some money for yourself.'

We rushed inside to look for old copies of the *Farmer's Weekly*. There must be ads in there, and sure enough there was an ad for Hy-Line Brown point-of-lay chickens.

'That's what you should do,' she said, 'buy those and sell the eggs.' Every little bit would help as I was battling to scrabble together enough money to survive each month. I was determined to keep up all my repayments, as I didn't want to ruin my own credit rating. John's was ruined already. I had accepted that, but it was becoming more and more difficult to cover all my own bills. I had a set salary that only stretched so far and, committed as I was to paying for the farm, there was very little left over for living expenses. If I had known John wasn't going to be back when I expected him, I would have rented a bachelor flat and tried to get back on my feet instead of having to cover the running costs of two houses, not to mention insurances, electricity and water. Luckily, I had a company car and petrol so all that I really needed in addition was some money for food, but there were many days towards the end of the month when the money had run out and dry crackers were all I had left to eat.

Laughing at our clever new scheme, Pam and I phoned the number in the magazine advertising Hy-Line Brown chickens. Yes they had thirty for us; we could pick them up next weekend at a cost of R420. The lady on the phone was very helpful and gave us the rate of lay we could expect and the quantities of feed and laying mash that would be needed each week, fifty kilograms of each. We were delighted and toasted our new scheme with some cheap red plonk.

We arranged to collect the chickens the following week on our way to the farm. They came in several cardboard boxes with ventilation holes. Pam and I placed them on the back seat, giggling and shrieking as they kept pushing up the lids, trying to escape. There was no getting away from it, neither of us was a real farming type!

Back in town, my friends were tasked with collecting egg boxes and every week we would go to the farm to collect the eggs and drive carefully back to Johannesburg with them. I would then sell them at the office, most of my colleagues being more than happy to have the opportunity to buy free-range eggs. The only problem was that they often didn't have cash with them so would casually say that they would pay me the following week, oblivious of the fact the R48 I was making from the eggs each week was needed to make ends meet. I kept up such a facade of being all right that very few people were aware of the seriousness of my financial situation. I was living a lie, pretending to cope during the day but giving into despondency and despair every night, crying myself to sleep in the dinginess of my new home.

So life carried on and I got into the routine of being a chicken farmer, the visit to the farm once a week helping me recharge my batteries for the difficulties of the week ahead. The farm was a place of refuge and renewal for me. It helped me come to terms with what was happening in my life and to look for ways of dealing with it. I had the opportunity to walk, always with a twig in my hand, up through the rocks and scrub over the hill to my own special rock, facing the Magaliesburg range of mountains. There I would sit for hours, gazing into the distance, thinking my thoughts, talking to myself and starting to work out what my next move should be.

It was at the farm that I started writing a journal, initially to remember all the things that had happened while John was away so that I wouldn't forget to tell him about them on his return. Then, eventually, it became an opportunity to record my thoughts and feelings as the realisation that he wasn't coming home began to sink in. The last straw had been the arrival of the latest Diner's Club statement. I had spent nothing that month, but John's charges were still coming through. At least it meant he was still alive, moving around Australia, but was it really necessary to spend so much money in restaurants? I was lucky if I could afford to eat, living mostly on bread and cheese, yet it looked like he was having a fine old time, living it up, eating out. I looked at the charges, *Gran Caffe, Jun Japanese Restaurant, Pasini's, Pinocchio's, Fiorelli's*. They didn't seem like the charges of someone who was living frugally. My patience was wearing thin and indignation at the way John was treating me started to set in. I had always been a good wife to him, loving and supportive, despite everything that had happened. He said he loved me and I believed him, but then, why was he doing this to me? The entries in my diary became more agitated as I started to rebel against the situation, bemoaning the fact that I had no way of fixing things. I just had to find him and sort this out.

I despaired at what the future would hold. There was no sign of John, his creditors were closing in. Everything looked impossible. Why had he left me with this mess? I had never known anything like this. My parents had always taught us to be responsible with money and to keep debt to a minimum and now here I was being hounded for money, which I hadn't even spent and which I didn't have and living in a dump which I couldn't fix.

I definitely had to do something about the gaping hole in the back door in the Regents Park house, as I was sure that I was hearing the sound of rats coming in and out in the middle of the night, the sight of their droppings on the kitchen floor greeting me every morning. When I had last spoken to John on my birthday he had said I should not do anything to fix up the house until he returned, but I started to realise that I had to at least do some things to make the place seem more homely. I couldn't relax surrounded by all the dust and decay. Besides it had been a good six months ago and I hadn't heard anything from him since.

I had no idea what was going on. I didn't know what to do, or where to contact him. My whole life was collapsing around me. He had said he would be back, where was he? He knew I needed him and must have known the kind of financial difficulties I was experiencing. Why had he not come home when he said he would? What on earth was happening? My anger that he had saddled me with so many problems became mixed with concern. Could something dreadful have happened to him?

Steve's funeral

'I need some time off on Thursday; I have to go to a funeral', I said to John Raath, my boss.

'What time is it?' He asked.

'Eleven o'clock.'

'That's fine, so you should be back for our meeting at 3 p.m.'

'I don't think so,' I responded. 'This is an Irish funeral so there will be a wake afterwards, it will probably go on until evening.'

'Fine,' was his reply, but he looked startled, the idea of celebrating death totally alien to him.

I had received a call from my friend Joan a few days earlier. Steve, our mutual friend, had been killed in a car accident. He had driven right under a stationary truck on the highway, killing himself instantly and leaving his wife, Wendy, with two small children, Robert who wasn't even a year old and Tara who was three. We had known Wendy and Steve for many years, seeing them regularly at the Irish Club in Hillbrow. Wendy was South African and Steve was from Northern Ireland. He had played the pipes at our wedding.

I was devastated. Poor Wendy, she idolised Steve. I couldn't imagine how she would manage without him. It made me realise that, difficult as my situation was, it could be a lot worse. I phoned her to offer my sympathy. She was trying to be brave but you could hear the strain in her voice.

Nigel phoned me a short while later to see if I had heard the news. He sounded really upset, he had liked Steve. We agreed to meet at the church and go in together. I had been avoiding most Irish get-togethers since John had gone away, finding it hard to cope with the endless questions about his whereabouts and the furtive glances in my direction to check how I was doing. I knew everyone meant well, but it upset me.

I left the office on the morning of the funeral, agreeing to meet Nigel outside the church. I would feel more comfortable going in with someone. I looked anxiously up and down the street for his van. I didn't want to face everyone on my own. They started to go into the church and still no sign of him. If he wasn't there in a minute I would have to go in by myself. Just as I was moving towards the church I saw his blue van in the distance. He was lucky and found parking quickly, hurrying to join me.

The service was in a Presbyterian church as Steve was Protestant. It was short, Wendy sitting in the front of the church with her family and Steve's family who had come over from Ireland.

After the service we made our way to West Park cemetery. There were so many cars in the funeral procession; Steve had been really well liked in the Irish community. It had been agreed that a Gospel Hall minister would say a few words at the graveside. He decided to use the opportunity to harangue us for our godlessness. He shouted fire and brimstone as an embarrassed silence descended on the group of mourners. We were going to go straight to hell, we were living such bad lives, there was little hope for any of us unless we saw the light and started to tread the right path. We didn't want to be disrespectful to Steve but this was inappropriate. I could see Wendy was losing control; this was not what Steve would have wanted, tears were streaming down her face. Finally, Craig drowned out the preacher's voice by playing the bagpipes, and the burial continued. I felt so sad for Wendy, a small, broken figure just trying to hold on and get through the day. She greeted everyone shakily and encouraged them to go to the wake.

I stood at the graveside afterwards paying my last respects to Steve. I wished John at least knew what had happened to his friend. Nigel had wandered off to chat to some friends. I stood there, fighting back the tears, feeling so terribly alone. I knew John should have been there with me. I felt the reality of the situation very deeply. It was eight months since he had gone away, and I hadn't spoken to him for over six months. What made me think he was ever coming back?

Al, Joan's husband, spotted me, standing alone at the graveside, and seemed to understand my overwhelming loneliness. He said nothing, just walked over to me and crushed me in a bear hug. It was so good to feel the comfort of another human being. I held him tight and let the tears flow. 'Don't worry, it'll be ok,' Al said.

I doubted that it would be, but wanted to cling to the thought that everything would be all right and it was just a matter of time, there was no way John would not be home for Christmas.

 *Airport*

Flight QF 63 from Sydney had landed. I glanced at the arrivals board, just twenty minutes late this time. I straightened my floral skirt and adjusted my hair. I had to look my best. It was a warm December Saturday morning; an air of anticipation stirred in the arrivals hall, children dressed in their best, eagerly awaiting the arrival of Granny and Grandpa for Christmas. Some held welcome banners, others clutched bouquets of flowers, the whole place was abuzz.

I was excited too, but also apprehensive. It was now the third Saturday in a row I had come to the airport, each time convincing myself that John would be getting off the plane to surprise me for our eighth wedding anniversary and for Christmas. Almost nine months had gone by since he had left, almost enough time to have had a baby. He wouldn't even have known, what a thought, devastating indeed!

He always loved to surprise me, coming back unexpectedly from all over the country. I hadn't heard from him since April, but knew he wouldn't leave me on my own for Christmas, that was out of the question! Each Saturday Christmas came closer and my levels of anticipation grew higher.

I shuffled impatiently from foot to foot, I knew my sandals looked great but they weren't comfortable. Not too much longer, I thought as a pressure point started to throb on the side of my foot. At long last the passengers started to come through, a mix of young and old, some clearly Australian and others returning South Africans, tears flowing freely as families were reunited, hugs and kisses aplenty.

I could feel tears pricking at the back of my eyes; it was going to be so emotional when we were finally reunited. I always got teary in the arrivals hall, just with the sheer emotional energy of the place. The waiting crowds started to thin, almost everyone was through. I eyed an old man on the other side of the barrier, also waiting like me; he glanced impatiently one more time at his watch. As he looked up his eye caught that of a young man struggling with a heavy backpack. Probably his son. His face lit up, a broad smile encompassing it entirely. At long last, his expression said, as he gripped the young man in a tight, lengthy embrace.

I struggled to hold back the tears as I realised that John was not on this flight either. I tried my best to compose myself and look nonchalant as I approached the information desk. I knew from bitter experience that passenger information would only be confirmed once the plane had landed. 'Excuse me,' I said to the young girl manning the desk, 'could you please confirm for me if a John Monaghan was on board the flight from Sydney?'

'Just a minute,' she said as she smiled at me. 'I'll check in the system.'

I breathed deeply; maybe he had been delayed by customs. At least it was a different girl to the one who had been there last week; it was becoming quite humiliating. I was beginning to feel like such a loser.

'Please spell that for me,' she asked. 'I don't seem to see his name but maybe I have the wrong spelling.'

I spelled it out, 'M-O-N-A-G-H-A-N.'

'I'm afraid not ma'am,' she said with a slightly quizzical look. 'Are you sure you have the correct flight?'

I gave her a shaky smile, 'I must have mixed up the dates, thanks for your help.'

I bolted for the toilet, I felt so foolish. This was all so hopeless. Who was I trying to kid? John obviously wasn't coming home. I splashed water on my blotchy, tear-stained face, thinking, I must calm myself before I get into the car. The last straw would be to have an accident!

What gave me the notion that John was coming back? Hang on until New Year at least, a little voice answered. Don't give up until then, he promised he would be back. What reason have you got to doubt his word? I didn't have any, it was a fact. He had always kept his promises to me. I wouldn't give up on him too easily.

Two months earlier I had been to a conference where Judi Moreo, an American speaker, gave the keynote address. She told the story of her brother who had had a bad motorbike accident. He was crabby and difficult and day in day out she spent time talking to him, caring for him, only to receive abuse and sarcasm in response. This went on for months until one day he snapped and asked.

'Why do you keep coming back for more when all I do is give you grief?'

'Because you're worth it and I never give up on someone who is worth it.'

It felt as if she was talking directly to me. John was worth it, why should I give up on him so easily? I loved him despite everything and knew once we were together again everything would work out all right.

So it was that my pilgrimage to the airport continued for another four weeks, right into the New Year of 1994, when the seeds of doubt started to take hold of my heart.

Christmas

'What are you doing for Christmas? You can't be on your own moping around,' my friends said.

'Don't worry I'm going to ...' and then I would name a friend that they didn't know too well.

The truth was that I had no intention of going anywhere. I thought I had been clever enough to convince my friends that I did indeed have plans for Christmas while all the time avoiding socialising with anyone. John had been away since February and I had no clue where he was or even if he was alive. I still hung on to the firm belief that he would not leave me on my own for Christmas and I wanted to be home when he eventually managed to contact me. I knew he didn't have my address but I had made sure his family had it, so he could always find me through them or Kathryn. I wasn't in the mood for company so had shrugged off every attempt to include me in any Christmas festivities.

I didn't sleep well on Christmas Eve. So many memories filled my mind and stopped me sleeping. The last minute rush to Sandton City for presents, John creating havoc in the kitchen as he made the stuffing, the carols playing, the house full of friends, the sound of laughter filling the air. That is how Christmas was meant to be. The only other time we had been apart at Christmas was when John first came to South Africa, we'd both had a miserable time that year. I looked back at the letter he wrote me then and tried to understand what was happening now. How could things have gone so wrong? I thought, as I read the letter he had written to me all those years ago:

> *I'm very sorry that I couldn't be with you for Christmas, but I promise you that we will have many more Christmases together. Mary I love you very much and I want to marry you and I want us to live happily together until we get old. I don't want to spend any more time without you.*

He had promised to be with me, so where was he?

It was a relief when Christmas morning came. At least I had things to do now. I planned to go to 8 a.m. Mass in Braamfontein, it wouldn't be as crowded as the later Mass and hopefully it would calm me and give me strength to face the day ahead. I knew in my heart that John would not miraculously appear, but I was not in the mood to feign good humour by spending time with other people on such a difficult day. I knew I would not be able to keep up any pretence that I was all right and coping; it was just so much easier to avoid everybody and get through the day as best I could.

It was a bright sunny morning when I drove through to Braamfontein. The church was busy. It always was at Christmas and Easter, and I glanced at the other churchgoers, recognising some of the regulars. I didn't know them well enough to speak to them but it was comforting to see familiar faces. Today though, most of them were with extended families, grannies with grandchildren, children back from varsity joining their parents. It dawned on me that I was one of the few people there on my own.

Despite my sadness, the sound of familiar hymns and carols had a soothing effect on me. I was tearful but resolved to overcome my emotions. I lit a candle for John and prayed fervently that wherever he was, he was well and that somehow I would have the strength to survive the day.

When Mass was over I hurried to my car, anxious to get home. I had left the answering machine on and planned to leave it on for the whole day, everyone thought I was out anyway. I had piled my presents on my bed and now the time had come to open them. My friends had been thoughtful; I received gifts of candles, soaps, every kind of thing geared to relaxation and calm. Kathryn had sent me a variety of presents including a video of *Sister Act*, with Whoopi Goldberg; I might put that on later for some light relief.

I decided to phone Kathryn at about midday, I didn't want to phone her too early as she had never been a morning person, but if I left it too late she would have already left for lunch at our cousin Marian's house in Surrey. I psyched myself up to make the call, it was important that I sounded on top of things; I didn't want to worry her. I tried three times, but the international lines were busy. At long last on the fourth attempt the phone rang. I thanked her for my presents and wished her Happy Birthday; she had been a Christmas baby. She was anxious to know what I was doing that day; I lied to her as easily as I had lied to everyone else. She was happy that I had plans, knowing how hard it was for me. We spoke about this and that, and then I put the phone down.

Thank goodness for that, I thought, now I don't have to pretend to anyone; I can just wallow in my misery. I let the tears flow, wanting the day to drift by, and then I could pick up the pieces again and carry on. I changed into a scruffy, comfortable pair of shorts matched with a loose T-shirt, there was no reason to get dressed up. It was all such a contrast to Christmas Days in the past when the sounds of laughter filled the house. Lunch lasted for hours; it was something I looked forward to. There would be nothing similar today. I had bought some pork sausages and, if my appetite returned, the most I could anticipate was a sausage sandwich.

It was warm in the house but I didn't feel like sitting outside. I sat in the lounge trying to read a book and shut out my grotty surroundings. I had no money to start doing any renovations to the house so I could not make it more pleasant for myself; my heart wasn't in it anyway, the grimness of my surroundings clearly mirroring my state of mind. I was overwhelmed by everything and was finding it almost impossible to pull myself out of the quagmire of my circumstances. I gazed at the pages of the book but realised that I was taking nothing in. I was going to have to do something otherwise the day was never going to end.

I was startled by the sound of a knock at the door, who could it be? Surely not John. I rushed to the door spurred on by that irrational thought. I opened it to be greeted by Nigel, a look of concern on his face.

'I knew you weren't going out,' he said. 'I brought your present. I just wanted to see if you were all right.'

I nodded, unable to speak. We both knew that I was not all right; he knew me so well, he just had to take one look at me.

'I know you don't want to go anywhere, but you know you are welcome to join Anne and myself at home.'

'I know, I'm just such awful company right now.'

'I understand, I just wanted you to know that you are welcome if you change your mind.'

I knew I was, Nigel had been such a special friend to me over the past few months. He was there for me at every point along the way. He didn't have to say anything; he just knew what was on my mind. He had also lost someone he loved and respected. I knew he was battling to reconcile the image he had of John as someone he looked up to and emulated with the John who seemed to have deserted me. But had he? That question remained unanswered, tormenting me more than anything else.

Should I be upset because John had left me or upset because something terrible had happened to him? If only I had the answer to that question.

Nigel left to join Anne, his partner, and the rest of her family in Germiston. He had met her shortly after John had gone away; I was glad for him, he deserved to be happy. It was good that he had come. I didn't have to play any games with him, I could just be myself. I saw him off at the gate; he looked incredibly sad and pensive. I felt for him, he must feel so helpless, not being able to make it better. I could relate to that, not having control of the situation was what bugged me the most.

I went back into the house. I had had a glass of wine and Nigel a beer. His visit had settled me to an extent. I was now ready for my scrumptious sausage sandwich, a Christmas lunch of note. I put the wine back in the fridge, that was the first and the last drink I would have that day. I had a firm rule about drinking on my own, I was even more strict now that John had gone away as I knew how easy it would be to find oblivion in a bottle at the end of a tough day.

The rest of the day passed in a blur, some television, some reading and then the *Sister Act* video, the box of tissues always close at hand. I smiled to myself; if I survive this day I can survive anything, I thought. I need to start facing the future and doing something to make things better.

 *Interpol*

'I think you should talk to Kobus,' my boss Andre Leenen said to me. 'It is a year since John went away and you have had no contact with him in ten months, since your birthday last year.'

I was no longer seeing charges billed to our Diner's Club card, and had no way of knowing if John was alive or dead. The last charge appeared on a statement issued at the end of December 1993. My spirits had soared when I saw a charge for Qantas airline on it. Could this be his return flight, I thought to myself? They were soon dampened when, on investigation, I found it was a ticket for a trip to Bali. So much for him rushing home, it seemed like he was still intent on travelling the world. While financially I was happy not to have to cover any more charges on the card, I was worried at what had happened to him. We had agreed at the time he left that he would signal to me that he was all right by using the card periodically to help me track his progress around Australia. Now the charges had stopped coming through, reducing the amount I had to find each month to pay the Diners card bill, but increasing my worry about his well-being. His card was due to expire soon, letting me off the hook about making the decision to cancel it. My friends had kept telling me to stop his card to ease the burden on my finances, but I couldn't bring myself to do it, somehow it seemed like a betrayal. At the same time I was sick to death of eating beans on toast, cheese sandwiches and cream crackers, while paying for John's bar and restaurant bills, not to mention flights to exotic destinations.

The news at that time was full of reports of a series of murders happening in Australia dubbed 'The Hitchhiker Murders'. The hunt was on for a serial killer who was preying on hitchhikers. John was travelling across Australia, hitchhiking, so I became frantic with worry. I knew my work was suffering as I was finding it hard to concentrate, my hand often shaking so much that I couldn't hold a pen.

I appreciated Mr Leenen's concern. By now he was like a father figure to me, a serious man, an accountant, originally from Holland. He had been a guest at our wedding and frequently talked about the liveliness of an Irish wedding in comparison with the more stuffy ones he usually attended.

Kobus van der Mescht headed up our Fraud Unit at American Express; he had strong links to the police and Interpol, as American Express had to work closely with the police on cases from time to time. Kobus knew about my situation, as did most other people at American Express. Although I didn't talk about it openly, they were aware and were concerned about me. He knew the deputy director of Interpol well, a man by the name of Vic McPherson, based at Police Headquarters in Pretoria.

'I'll phone him and explain your problem,' he said. 'Then you can call him and make arrangements to see him.'

'Do you think he'll be able to help?' I asked quietly.

Was there something I could do to get on top of the situation at long last? I hated the feeling that I had no control over what was happening, the feeling that there was nothing I could do to resolve the situation; I hated the feeling of helplessness.

Two days later Kobus came past my desk.

'I spoke to Vic,' he said, 'he will be able to help you. Here's his number, please give him a call.'

Finally, some action, I thought to myself as I picked up the phone. I got through to him immediately, he sounded warm and friendly.

'I know you are based in Johannesburg,' he said, 'so why don't you come after work and we can see what we can do. Please bring as much information as you can and also a recent photograph if you have one.'

I arranged to meet him the next day. I left work half an hour early to miss the rush hour traffic. I had a file on the seat next to me, a photo of John taken the Christmas before he left and copies of the Diner's Club statements showing where he had been. It was all I had. When I looked at how sketchy it was, there wasn't much to go on.

Vic McPherson had told me to park across the road, in a public parking garage, the streets were deserted by the time I arrived. Johannesburg people joked that Pretoria closed down at 3.30 p.m. and it seemed true. Civil servants didn't seem to work long hours. I looked across at the grey building housing police headquarters. I felt uneasy entering the foyer, there was a distinct grimness about the place.

I asked for Vic McPherson at the security desk, completed the checking-in procedures and was let through the security gates to the lift. I felt uneasy, trapped, there was no quick way out of here, but I was here of my own free will, so what was my problem? I tried to push these thoughts out of my mind and took the lift up to the floor occupied by Interpol.

Vic McPherson met me at the door, a short middle-aged man with black hair, a beard and an easy smile. 'Come in', he said as he showed me into his office.

It was an old-fashioned place dominated by a large desk in dark wood and an executive chair. To the side there was a coffee table and two chairs. On the table were an arrangement of artificial flowers and a bible placed on top of a lace doily. These homely touches were at odds with the austerity of the rest of the office.

'Please sit down,' he said, gesturing towards the chairs by the coffee table. 'We'll be more comfortable here.' He had a soft, gentle voice. 'Now tell me your story and I'll see what I can do to help.'

I took him through the story of John's leaving, the minimal contact and then the silence. I told him of my fears that there could be a link to the hitchhiker murders. He nodded as I talked, occasionally saying, 'Yes I understand.' He seemed a kind man, easy to talk to.

'Why are you trying to find him?' he asked. 'We don't generally get involved in domestic issues. Are you wanting a divorce or to claim money from him?'

I assured him that I just wanted to know that he was all right, nothing more. There had been no reason to suspect he was not going to return, if that had been his intention I knew he would have taken some precious personal things with him, like the old biography of Michael Collins that I had had leather bound for him and which he cherished so much.

Vic explained that once someone is over twenty-one, and if they choose not to reveal their whereabouts, all Interpol can do is confirm that they are all right. They cannot reveal their contact details without permission. I was comfortable with that, why would John want to hide from me?

Then we got down to the business of my statement. He painstakingly took down every last detail, prompting me with questions which might help the investigation. Did John socialise? What kind of places would he frequent? He was clearly building up a profile of John in his mind.

'I will deal with this personally. It may take some time but I will not give up until I have some news for you. Phone me at any time if you want to see how we are doing. I will be in contact the minute I have something for you.'

He smiled at me, 'It must be very hard for you. God is good, it'll be ok.'

I smiled shakily. It had been draining to go through all the detail again, but I felt relieved that I was doing something at long last.

'Where have you parked?'

'Just across the road.'

'Are you all right walking across or shall I accompany you?'

I assured him I would be all right and thanked him for his kindness.

I was glad to escape the claustrophobic feel of the building and breathe in the air of the Pretoria streets. I felt exhausted, realising when I glanced at the clock in the car that I had been there for over two hours. No wonder I was shattered. I felt good though, optimistic that we would be able to find out something.

A month went by. Vic phoned me to say they had met several dead ends, but they were still working on John's case and to phone him any time if I thought of anything that might help. I had given him everything

I could and was hopeful it would be enough. How difficult could it be to find John? I tried to keep myself busy, working long hours to keep my impatience at bay. I forced myself not to phone and follow up, knowing Vic would tell me as soon as he had news. Two more months passed; I found it strange I hadn't heard anything. I couldn't sit around any longer, and I hated not being able to take control. That had been my problem all along, I felt helpless not being able to make things right. I phoned the number Vic had given me. Somebody else answered the phone.

'May I speak to Vic McPherson?' I asked.

'We have no one here by that name; he doesn't work here any more.'
I didn't know what to say, what could I do now? 'Is he working somewhere else? Is there anywhere I can contact him?'

'I have no further information,' the man at the other end of the line said curtly.

'Who's speaking?'

'Why are you looking for him? You are speaking to Lieutenant Rogers, I am handling his work.'

I explained how Vic had been helping me. 'Are you able to check on my case? I asked.

'We don't handle domestic cases,' he said. 'This is most irregular; we cannot help you unless it is a criminal matter.'

'But what about the possible link to the hitchhiker murders?' I stammered.

'No link has been established. We really can't help you.'

I could feel the tears welling up in my eyes.

'Please, you must help me. I don't know what to do.'

'I'll see what I can do,' he said begrudgingly, 'but I doubt we'll have any luck. If he doesn't want to be found it's unlikely we will find him. It's a long shot.'

'Will you contact me if you find anything?'

'Yes, I will, but don't get your hopes up.'

I had reached another dead end. The chances of Lieutenant Rogers doing anything to help seemed less than zero. I was back to where I started.

I let another month go by and decided to take the initiative and phone him again. I was greeted by a sigh of exasperation when he realised who it was and a curt dismissal of my enquiry. I wrote off any chance of finding John this way.

A week later, I got into the office from a meeting across town. Joey handed me a message, please phone Lieutenant Rogers. I gulped. I couldn't believe it, did he actually have news? I rushed into my office to phone, my hand shaking as I dialled the number.

'I have news for you,' he said triumphantly, 'we have located Mr Monaghan. He is well but says that everyone who needs to know his whereabouts does so. I am not at liberty to give you any details.' I could hear gloating in his voice. 'I did warn you,' he said. 'We have closed the case.'

I don't believe it, I thought, I just don't believe it. Why would he say that? How could John not want me to know where he is? I started to cry, it was so unfair. I needed to go home. I needed to work through this on my own, my mind was in turmoil. 'I'm leaving now,' I said to Joey, 'something has come up at home. I have a workshop at Helderfontein tomorrow, I'll see you on Thursday.'

I drove home talking to myself, unable to believe what had just happened. I let myself into the house in Regent's Park and the tears flowed as I paced round and round the bedroom trying to understand what had just happened and to come to terms with it. I felt as if I had been kicked in the stomach. What could I do now? All the while a niggling doubt remained at the back of my mind. Had they really found John or was this Lieutenant Rogers' way of getting an irritating female off his back? Yet another unanswered question.

'Are you alright?' Candida asked, as I took my place next to her at the conference in Helderfontein the next morning.

'Not really,' I said, 'I took the wrong turn and then bumped into another car as I was reversing down the dirt road. I'm just a bit shaky, that's all.' Who was I trying to kid? That was an understatement. I hardly remembered the drive to the venue, I hadn't slept at all the night before, my hands were shaking uncontrollably, my head was throbbing, and I couldn't focus on anything. Now what? I kept asking myself. You've got to do something; you can't go on like this, you're a mess.

New beginnings

Little by little I got together enough money to start fixing up my house, helped by the sale of eggs and wood from the farm. It was still not the best but it was at least habitable. A year had gone by since I had moved in and at least I could sit there in the evening with some level of comfort, but the area was bad and the neighbours were messy and noisy. I never really felt safe, but knew I couldn't afford the prices of houses anywhere else.

In October 1994 I managed to go on holiday to Umhlanga on the Natal coast with Helga, another friend from American Express. She was older than me, German, but had lived in South Africa for over twenty years, never losing her strong German accent. She had worked for American Express for many years, starting out in the travel side and then moving through to Card Division. We had booked one of the Nedbank company flats, the rate was cheap and we could drive down with my company car so it really wasn't going to be any more expensive than being at home, or so we convinced ourselves. The plan was to relax, tanning ourselves on the beach and just generally taking it easy.

'You can't go on like this,' Helga said as she poured me a glass of wine. 'You need to get out and start seeing other men.' She settled into the armchair next to me and lit up one of her favourite long, thin cigarettes. We had known each other for years, since 1983 when I had first started to work for American Express.

'You need a man in your life,' Helga said, 'you are young and attractive, you can't sit around on your own forever, you'll end up like a dried-up old prune. It's not natural for you to be on your own, you need to get out and meet men.'

'But I can't,' I replied. 'You know I am still married, it's not right for me to go out with anyone while I am still married.'

'I know how you feel but it's not helping you. If you can't face a permanent relationship why don't you just have sex with someone, a one-night stand, it will do you the world of good.'

I could see she wasn't joking; she leaned over to me and looked me in the eye, 'You know you need to do something.'

I glanced down, embarrassed, how could I possibly contemplate such a thing, it would be so out of character for me. What was she thinking?

'Just imagine how good it would feel to have someone to hug and touch you, the warmth of another human being next to you in bed.'

She had hit a nerve. I so longed to be touched, John and I had always held and hugged each other so much and I missed it terribly.

She could see I was wavering. 'No one needs to know. Just do what you need to do. You don't even have to tell me. It'll make you feel so much better; all you have to do is send me a postcard. You don't need to write anything, a blank postcard, addressed to me, and then I'll know.'

I smiled shyly, maybe she had a point, and it was about time I started breaking out. All my life I had done the right thing but where had it got me? Besides it wasn't as if John had been faithful, why shouldn't I find happiness somewhere else?

'Come on,' she said, 'drink up, we'll be late for dinner.'

I gathered up my things and headed for the door.

Did I ever send Helga a postcard? Eventually yes, but only many years later. Was it worth the wait? Most definitely.

Our holiday in Umhlanga was nearly over as we lazed around in the flat reading.

'Mary, have you seen this ad?' Helga said, passing the Sunday paper over to me.

I glanced at the paper. The advertisement was for a Customer

Financial Services Manager; the description it gave exactly matched my experience.

'Look at the salary,' she said with a grin.

'Wow, it's so much more than I am getting now.'

'Maybe it's worth a try.'

'Maybe,' I said, trying to sound nonchalant but quietly imagining how all that extra money would help.

I worked with Helga, so was a little bit wary of committing to apply for the job in front of her, but that night, after a light supper and a few glasses of wine, I retrieved the careers section of the newspaper from the waste bin and put it in my bag. I should think about it, maybe it was time for a change. I had been thinking of changing jobs for some time, especially since I had recently finished an Executive Development course. I had worked in Customer Services at American Express Card for ten years and was starting to get bored with what I was doing. I had already discussed this with my boss, John Raath.

'An Executive Development Course may be the way to go,' he had said to me. 'We can nominate one person to attend per year; the idea is to improve their all round strategic business knowledge to prepare them for more responsibility or possibly a change in position. It's hard work but very interesting and stimulating. Unfortunately, we have already nominated someone to go on this year's one but maybe next year.'

I was disappointed because once I get an idea about doing something I like to get on with it straight away, but I put it at the back of my mind and carried on as usual.

Two months later John Raath had called me into his office.

'Mary, we spoke a few months ago about the EDP course. Gavin was nominated to do it but with the launch of the new Megalink Card he won't be able to attend. He received his books for pre-reading a few months ago. If you stepped in, it would mean that you would have a lot of catching up to do in time for the start of the course in April, what do you think?'

I jumped at the chance. 'I've never been frightened of hard work,' I said.

'I'll do the necessary paperwork and get Gavin to send the box of books over to you.'

Just what I needed, a new challenge. As always, I stuck to my study plan religiously, if I had to read all of this by April I certainly would do so.

As the April deadline loomed, I started to get nervous. How would I fit in with the rest of the banking delegates, as I had no formal business education? How would my degree in French and Spanish help? Not a lot I feared. Then I remembered what my mother had always said: 'Remember you are as good as anyone else; and can do anything you set your mind to.' The thought of her saying this to me gave me renewed confidence.

The course was being held at the Riverside Sun at Vanderbijlpark, the starting date being a few days after the first democratic elections in 1994.

My friend Lynn had suggested I pop round and see her after I had voted. I had gone to the polls quite early with Sarah, but still there were long queues and talk on the radio of extending the voting for another day to give everyone a chance to cast their vote. It was quite a sight to see, queues and queues of people of all colours, waiting patiently in line to vote together on this special day. A mood of excitement and camaraderie filled the air, everyone good humoured, revelling in the fact that this was an historic day. Who would have thought even five years ago that Sarah and I would be standing together in a queue, waiting to vote?

I knocked on Lynn's door. 'Here I am, have you voted?'

'We're going later,' she said, her mouth dropping open at the sight of me on her doorstep. I hadn't washed my hair; it hung straggly and unkempt around my face. I was wearing an old pair of jeans with a faded stained sweatshirt, which had seen better days. It was hanging on me as I had lost so much weight in the last few months. My skin was grey and wrinkled from lack of sleep. I hadn't seen Lynn for some time, we had both been busy. We had been friends from the time I arrived in South Africa, as Lynn's ex-husband, Jimmy, and John became friends soon after John arrived in South Africa. They had worked together on a project on Western Deep Levels mine in Carletonville.

'Come in, come in,' she said, as I went into the lounge to greet Paul her husband. 'Sit down, would you like some coffee?'

'Yes, please.'

She looked flustered as if she didn't quite know how to handle me. She had never seen me like this; I always gave the impression of being in control.

'Are you all right?' she said quietly as she poured the coffee.

'Not really,' I replied as I swallowed back the tears. The year since John had gone had definitely taken its toll.

My birthday just a few days previously had brought no word from John. It was a year since I had heard his voice, when he had left me the message on my answering machine, wishing me happy birthday. I had played the tape again this year, just to feel that he was thinking of me wherever he was. I was battling to survive financially, and emotionally I was a mess. I just couldn't accept the fact that he was not coming back, there was no reason for him to disappear, he had planned to come back and renovate the house.

'You can't go on like this,' she said, 'you'll get sick.'

'I'm trying,' I replied 'but it's just so hard. Maybe the course will take my mind off it. It is supposed to be hard work; I won't have too much time to think.'

We spoke for an hour or two and I left feeling a lot calmer. I now needed to get home and start packing some clothes for the time away. Maybe Lynn is right, I thought, I need to have a good break.

The course started on a Sunday. We had to check in on the Sunday afternoon. During the lectures the dress code was smart casual but they also had said that the opening dinner was smart, suits for men, so I packed accordingly, I didn't want to be caught out. I set off on a beautiful Highveld autumn day, Vanderbijlpark wasn't too far from me and I always enjoyed a drive out of town. My little white Opel hummed along the highway.

I pulled up at the hotel, a little apprehensive, what was I letting myself in for? Would I be able to cope? Relax, I told myself. Easier said than done, of course. The young hotel student behind the desk smiled at me.

'Are you part of the Nedcor Group?'

'Yes I am.'

'Please sign here and I will get a porter to help you with your luggage.' I followed the porter along the corridor to the room at the very end of the passage. He stood back to let me in, taking time to show me all the facilities and how to use the TV remote.

'Enjoy your stay!' He said and let himself out.

I bounced on the bed, it seemed comfortable at least. I checked to see if the pillows were feather. I was allergic to feather pillows and it was always better to check early before I forgot and woke up from a deep sleep with bags like golf balls under my eyes. No, safe enough, plain old synthetic!

I arranged my books neatly on the desk and looked at the timetable for the next week. It was going to be hectic. We were divided into syndicate groups of four. I glanced at the list of names, it didn't tell me anything. I did notice that out of thirty delegates there were only two women, that was going to be interesting. I lay down on the bed and took a deep breath. This is a chance to prove yourself, I said quietly, and nobody knows you, so enjoy it!

I spent the next hour watching the end of a trashy movie, killing time before I showered and changed for the introductory formal dinner. I didn't want to get there too early and have no one to talk to. It would be mostly men so I wouldn't wear anything too obvious. Understated elegance should be the way to go. Black is always good, with discreet jewellery, that's what my mother had always said anyway. She would have been so proud to see me attending a course like this, I thought as I arrived at the reception area to collect my name tag.

I walked into the ballroom to be greeted by a sea of dark suits and ties, not a woman in sight. I took a deep breath, clutched the glass of sweet sherry that had been thrust at me and walked into the fray, my head held high. I was immediately greeted by one of the administrators who introduced me to some of my fellow delegates. It was easier than I had imagined; after all, none of us knew each other so we were all in the same boat.

We talked superficially, the usual cocktail conversation. Where are you from? What do you do? Are you married? Children, the weather and so it continued. The time came to be seated at our designated tables ready for the start of the formal proceedings. Various academics from the University of Stellenbosch Business School were there – and so the speeches began. I glanced around at the other seven people seated at my table and the rest of the room and suddenly felt my throat go dry, my heart started to thump. I felt a flush rise on my cheeks. I need air; I need to get out of here, I thought, as I headed for the cloakrooms. There I splashed cold water on my face, took deep breaths and tried to calm down. This is a great start, I thought to myself, as I looked at my frightened face in the mirror. A few minutes went by and

I felt calmer. Time to go back in, I said, they'll be wondering what has happened to you. I walked back in; no one so much as glanced at me, not having noticed that I had gone. I felt better, the moment had passed. I smiled at my dinner companions as the small talk started once more.

The next day lectures began and they were more interesting than I had imagined. I had never been exposed to business-orientated subjects. We worked hard but we played too. I was starting to relax in the company of all these men. I was enjoying all the attention I was receiving too, especially as my fellow delegates were interacting with me as a person in my own right. I wasn't poor Mary, the deserted wife, nor were they interested in whether I had heard from John. They accepted me for who I was, it felt so liberating. I was an independent woman, no longer just the other person in a relationship. I was starting to recover my identity and rebuild my confidence, I had always been a bright, capable woman, but somehow that side of me had got lost along the way. I had spent most of the last years playing a support role to John. I felt I was blossoming; they were unknowingly nurturing my fragile spirit and helping me to find myself again.

I was particularly friendly with the delegates from the coastal areas, Port Elizabeth, Durban and Cape Town. We often walked down to the river together at night and talked about everything imaginable in relaxed companionship. Too soon the two weeks were over and it was time to go back to the real world. We had to spend time now doing assignments before meeting up again in August, in Cape Town.

'You look great,' said Lynn whom I had arranged to meet soon after at Gino's for supper. 'There's something different about you. Have you done something to your hair?'

'No,' I said but I excitedly told her all about my two weeks away, the words tumbling out.

'You're so bubbly,' she said, 'I didn't think I would ever see you like this again. Paul and I were so worried about you on Election Day, you looked dreadful.'

'I feel like a new person,' I said, grinning from ear to ear. 'I know now that I can survive this, I will get through. I know it won't be easy but I will do it.'

She reached for my hand. ' I'm so glad,' she said, 'you deserve to be happy again.'

The next months were busy ones. The writing of assignments was not something I really enjoyed, seeing it as a necessary evil. I enjoyed the interaction of lectures and syndicate groups far more. At last all my assignments were submitted and I could start preparations for my time in Cape Town. I was looking forward to seeing everyone again; we had created strong bonds of friendship. This time we were housed at the University of Stellenbosch Business School, Bellville campus, not the most exciting venue in Cape Town but close enough to visit central Cape Town if need be. Again I blossomed in the company of my new friends, dealing with complex business issues but finding time to social-ise too.

We worked hard, even more so than in the original study block, but we were determined to enjoy the Cape Town nightlife as well. All too soon it was over, a gala dinner at the Cape Sun and then we went our separate ways.

I had decided to spend some extra time in Cape Town. I was booked in at the Arthur's Seat Hotel in Seapoint. My boss at Card Division had agreed to pay for my accommodation as I was going to visit some Nedbank branches on the Monday and Tuesday.

'Hope you don't mind,' Pam Davies said to me, 'but we have to go to Atlantis, I have an appointment with the manager there.'

'That's fine, but where is Atlantis?'

'It's up the West Coast, past Blauuwberg.'

I was relaxed, not minding where we went; besides I always liked to discover new places. The Cape West Coast was a whole new world to me, not the picture-postcard beauty of the Cape that I had previously seen. The barrenness of the landscape with its sparse vegetation sprout-ing up from the dunes and its wildness and desolation awoke memories in me of the West of Ireland where my parents had been born. There was something about its savage beauty that resonated with me, I felt at home and embraced by its beauty.

'I'll be back,' I said to Pam as we drove back to Cape Town, 'the West Coast is very special, it touches my soul.'

Grotto Bay

A few weeks later, back in Johannesburg, I glanced at the property section in the *Business Day*. There was a Cape property supplement that week. I had always fancied living somewhere by the coast but money was still such a problem. A full-page ad for a coastal development on the West Coast at Grotto Bay caught my eye. Plots starting from 55,000 rands, that wasn't too bad, not that I had that kind of money but I just needed the deposit and maybe I would get a good year-end bonus from work. A bond for the balance might just be manageable once I got my annual increase. It said only 220 houses would be built to strict design specifications. It looked interesting. I dialled the number; there was no harm in enquiring and, after all, it was always good to dream. They said they would send me the documentation. Eventually it arrived and I read through it excitedly, it looked wonderful.

'It's a shame it is so far away as I would need to see it to make a decision,' I said to Pam as I showed her the brochures.

It was an impossible dream, and there was no way I could get to fulfil it. Grotto Bay – it's great to dream, I thought to myself as I put the brochures away.

One evening in November Pam and Uwe joined me for a simple supper of Irish stew. The weather had turned unusually cold and besides it was a good cheap meal. Uwe bent as he came through the door. He was a bear of a man, a tall bearded German, and strongly built, in his fifties and a friend of Pam's for many years. The conversation flowed easily over the stew and red wine. Uwe was an architect, so Pam started to tell him about Grotto Bay.

'Get the information out,' she ordered. 'Let Uwe have a look at it.'

I passed him the brochures. With true German precision he took time to digest all the information before pronouncing judgement.

'It looks great,' he said, 'but you would have to go there to check it out.'

'I know, but I can't afford the flight.'

'Let's think of going in December. We can drive down together, then it won't be so expensive.'

We agreed that his would be the best course of action. I was just impatient though. What if all the plots had been sold? But I was also a great fatalist, so I had to allow fate to take its course. Besides, I had no idea where I would get the money from anyway.

'Have you heard any more about that job you applied for in Cape Town?' Pam asked.

'Not a word,' I said.

It seemed a lifetime since I had seen the *Sunday Times* ad in Umhlanga with Helga in September. On arriving back, I got out the ad from my suitcase where I had hurriedly stuffed it. They needed a CV and I hadn't put one together for years. I wasn't the greatest typist either, and the only people I could call on to help were from American Express so that wouldn't help much, as I didn't want them to know what I was doing.

I phoned Peter to see if he had any bright ideas. I had met him at Wendy's house shortly after Steve died. Peter and his brother John lived next door, and had been towers of strength after Steve passed away. They helped Wendy with the children and were always available to assist her with anything she needed. I got to know both John and Peter well, they were young and single but more than happy to help where they could. I visited Wendy frequently after Steve's death and we became closer than ever before, partly as a result of our both finding ourselves suddenly on our own.

I took Peter through the basics and he said he would work on the CV with Wendy for me. The next day, true to his word, it was ready. I went round to his house to pick it up.

'I hope you don't mind, I got a bit creative when it came to interests, I added that you had an interest in wildlife. I'm sure they wouldn't think for a minute I was referring to your chicken farming exploits!'

I sent off my CV the next day and promptly forgot about it. The job was not quite what I was doing but I did have the mix of experience they were looking for. The ad had explained that they needed someone to look at credit from a service perspective. It was quite an innovative approach but made a lot of sense to me.

Ten days later I received a phone call from a firm of consultants inviting me for an interview at Gilbeys in Midrand. I arranged to be there two days later in my lunchtime, anticipating that the interview would not last too long. In the end I was out of the office for three hours. It was unusual for me to go out at lunchtime, and I could see other people in the office were curious as to where I had been but I kept a low profile. It had been a tough interview. I had no idea how I had done but at least it was good to give it a try.

I decided nothing was going to come of it as it had been over a month since the interview and I had heard nothing more, so much for a change of direction. Just when I had given up, a call came through.

'Are you able to speak now?'

'Yes, it is fine.'

'We would like you to come to our offices in Stellenbosch for a meeting. Would Wednesday be all right?'

'I think so; I will just have to check about taking some time off.'

'Please get back to me as soon as possible, as we need to arrange your travel booking.'

'Ok, I'll get back to you this afternoon.'

I nearly leapt out of my chair with excitement. Just last night I had been sitting in my tumbledown house in Regent's Park, discussing a trip to Cape Town with Pam and Uwe. This had to be fate. Now I had the means to get to Grotto Bay. I asked for two days leave, one to attend the interview and one for a recce of Grotto Bay. I just had to tell Pam.

'I'll phone Uwe,' she said, 'he'll have to mark which plots you need to look at.'

He marked the plots and gave me strict instructions to take photos from various angles to help us make the right decision.

I phoned Nicky, the estate agent. 'I'll be there on Thursday,' I said.

'Great, I'll work out which plots are still available in your price range.'

I was excited, what if this job came through? I would have more money every month and on top of that I could use my pension money to buy the plot. I popped out at lunchtime to attend the 1 o'clock mass at the church in Braamfontein. Lighting a candle, I prayed fervently that things would take a turn for the better, 'Please God, let this happen; let me have the chance to start afresh.'

I dressed carefully for the interview. I was flying in early in the morning and would be collected at the airport and driven through to Gilbeys in Stellenbosch. The Finance Director was interviewing me; he was tall, blonde and quite reserved. I found him intimidating. 'What do you think you have to offer us?' he asked abruptly.

I proceeded to tell him. He seemed distracted, uncomfortable in an interview for this new kind of position. It lasted about forty-five minutes and at the end I wasn't too sure how it had gone, he was a difficult person to read. If all else fails at least I've had my trip to Cape Town paid for, I thought. They dropped me at Avis at the airport, where I picked up the car which I would use to go to Grotto Bay the next day.

I checked into the hotel, got out the brochures and rechecked what I needed to investigate the next day. Uwe's instructions were very clear. He had left nothing to chance. I arranged to meet Nicky at 10 am; she had given me directions to Grotto Bay, 'Take the R27 West Coast road, after Atlantis it will be another fifteen minutes drive. The turn-off is to the left.'

It was a beautiful early summer's day as I drove along, humming to the music on the radio, feeling glad to be alive. Forty-five minutes after leaving Cape Town I saw the sign, 'Grotto Bay, Where the Whales

Play'. I turned onto the gravel road. Just as I turned a tortoise crossed the road in front of me. Now this has to be a sign, I said to myself. I had started to collect tortoises when we were on honeymoon and now had a collection of at least forty – china, wood, soapstone, in every shape and size. I was convinced that seeing a tortoise was a good omen.

I pulled up at the wooden sales office and Nicky bounded out – a short, bubbly, middle-aged lady who greeted me with a broad smile. 'I've worked out the plots in your price range,' she said to me.

'That's great; I know exactly which ones I am interested in.'

'How much time do you have?'

'My flight is only in the early evening so we can take our time.'

We started at the close furthest from the sales office, driving along gravel roads to get there. There were only a handful of homes built at the time so it all looked very isolated. The sun shone on a clear blue sea, waves crashing on the rocks in the bay.

I thought to myself, I can live here. Please God it works out.

At each of the designated plots on Uwe's list I first took a photo of the plot number board, followed by shots from various angles as instructed. There were only three or four plots that looked like good possibilities and as I spoke to Nicky she was full of good advice too, taking into consideration the size of the clusters and the angle of the plot. I couldn't afford one of the front plots, they were definitely out of my reach financially, but there were a couple further back which caught my eye.

Eventually, we narrowed the choice down to plot nos. 122 and 113, but in my heart 122 was the one I felt would be best.

'Let's have a last look at both,' Nicky suggested as we drove around once more.

'Plot 122 will always have a good view of the sea because of the open space in front of it – but show it to your friend with the photos of the other ones and see what he thinks. There is no hurry, get back to me when you are ready.'

I smiled to myself. I will do this if it takes every cent that I have, I thought. This place is so beautiful and unspoilt I feel at home here already.

I said goodbye to Nicky and drove away from the sales office, but I couldn't tear myself away from Grotto Bay. I headed down to the point, just at the end of the main gravel road, parked my car and gazed at the sea. I took a few deep breaths and could feel a stillness come over me. It's so good for the soul, I thought, I will have to find a way to make this happen.

Finally, I had to tear myself away and leave for the airport to catch my flight home. Brimming with stories to tell everyone when I got back, I felt more alive than I had for years. I could feel that Grotto Bay was going to help me get my life back on track. My visit to the Gilbeys' offices in Stellenbosch made me start to consider that the job could actually be a possibility. I met Peter and Wendy for dinner soon after I returned from Cape Town and told them all about my interview and my recce to Grotto Bay. The words tumbled out; no matter what happened, life had started to take an interesting turn.

Two days later another call came through. I was invited to yet another meeting, this time at Midrand. That's great, all my friends said excitedly, a third interview; it will probably be a formality, a chance to discuss salary. Not wanting to leave anything to chance, I arrived ten minutes early, just as a blonde lady was being shown out. So it wasn't just me. So much for being a rubber stamp. I was wearing an olive green suit which ended just above my knees. I walked into the office, to find it full of people, a panel of six and to top it all I had to sit on a low couch, not the most genteel way to have to sit, dressed as I was. I was introduced to the panel; representatives from Human Resources, Sales, Finance, Distribution. My heart sank. I wasn't prepared for this. They fired questions at me. I settled into the interview, I was here now and would just have to make the most of it; all I could do was my best. I took a deep breath and started to relax. The questions weren't so bad. I started to enjoy myself, and emerged an hour later, drained but satisfied that I had given it my best shot.

'We'll get back to you next week,' James McLachlan, my potential boss, said to me, smiling reassuringly. He was tall and thin, with an unruly mop of hair and a beard. He had a nice easy manner, not a bit like the accountants I was used to in the banking environment.

'I'll be in Namibia,' I replied, 'doing some training.'

'Please leave your contact details with my secretary so we can contact you.'

'Ok,' I replied, heaving a sigh of relief that I had survived the interview.

'So much for rubber-stamping,' I said to Peter as I phoned him from the office. 'I was grilled again.'

'I'm sure you impressed them,' he replied.

'Of course,' I said, laughing.

'When do you leave for Namibia?'

'Monday, I can't wait. I'm travelling all over, visiting the bank branches, it'll be great. I'm hoping to catch up with Monique, remember her, my friend from Amex in Windhoek. She's going to take me to Joe's Beer Hall; apparently it's great fun there. I'll let you know if I have any news from Gilbeys.'

My trip to Windhoek was hectic but I did manage to spend time with Monique. I had been there for three days already and still no word. Then, on the third evening, I got back to the hotel to find there was a message for me to phone Gilbeys. I tried the number. It was too late, and James McLachlan had already left. The time difference between the two countries didn't help and it was before the era of cell phones, so during office hours I had no opportunity to call. I missed James three times over the next days; eventually his secretary, Judy, took pity on me and gave me the good news. I'd got the job.

I was offered the position starting in January 1995, at a salary that represented a substantial increase from what I had been earning. With the increase and the money I was able to withdraw from my Pension fund I would be able to buy a plot at Grotto Bay. My dream of building there could come true. Things were now starting to come together. My life was changing, a new job, a new project to keep me busy. But still there were always questions at the back of my mind. Where was John and was he ever going to come back?

I didn't have to build at Grotto Bay immediately. The only regulation was that of having to complete one's place within one year of starting to build. I was keen to get going though. The great thing was that now

I had to come to Stellenbosch for meetings at least once a month, so I could always visit Grotto Bay and see what was happening.

Uwe was tasked with drawing the plans for the house; he usually drew plans for office buildings, so this was a new challenge for him. I asked him what he would like as payment and he asked for a couple of weekends at the house when it was completed. I left it at that. I would have been more comfortable paying my way but he was adamant. I was very specific about what I wanted so we often locked horns about my 'unreasonableness'. I had never been the most practical of people, always looking at things from a more romantic angle. I just had to have a bath that looked to the sea; there was no question about this, despite the fact that it caused untold problems with the planning of the plumbing – and so it went on. Many nights were spent poring over plans, Pam and I, giving Uwe grey hairs with our endless ideas.

The plans were now finished and the time had come to get quotes for the building works. We had a fair idea of what the going rate was, bearing in mind that Grotto Bay was isolated and only practical for builders from the Atlantis and Darling areas. The quotes started to come in for almost double what I had anticipated. I phoned the builders in desperation, trying to understand what was going on. 'It's the design,' they all said, 'it is too complex, the roof structure alone needs so much work.'

How could I tell Uwe that his design was causing problems? This was not going to be the easiest of things; he was inflexible to say the least and would not take kindly to his work being questioned. The issue of the design heralded the end of our friendship to the point that he threatened to sue me for the cost of drawing the plans, but I was not prepared to compromise on my dream. Now I had to go to plan B.

One of the delegates from my EDP course, Allan Brown, lived in Cape Town. He told me of an architect, Ronell Ackermann, whom he had used for renovations to his house. She was from Durbanville and would probably be able to assist me. On my next trip to Cape Town I arranged to meet her. I went to her office in Durbanville and she sat down with me and asked me to explain how I saw my dream West Coast Irish cottage. I gave her a few of my ideas.

'Is it a bit like this?' She asked, handing me a book.

'Yes it is,' I replied, quite startled as I realised the book was full of pictures of Mediterranean cottages. I hadn't realised before, but in my mind the Irish cottage image had merged with memories of Cyprus, which I remembered from my childhood there.

'Give me three weeks,' she said 'and I will have something for you.'

Indeed she did and it was just what I was looking for. Small and simple, but with some interesting nooks and crannies giving a special feel to the place. I could now explain to her the dilemma I had with finding suitable builders and she told me of one young builder she knew who didn't have too much experience but was full of good ideas. That was how I came into contact with Deon.

Deon was just starting out, a young Afrikaans builder coming from Somerset West, full of energy, passion and ideas; very different to any of the builders I had come into contact with in Gauteng. Blonde hair held back in a ponytail, piercing blue eyes and a surfer's body to boot, he was charming and funny and made our meetings a mixture of business and fun.

I was in no rush to finish the house. I had limited funds and, of course, with me based in Johannesburg, building at a distance was always going to be a challenge. Add to this the fact that Deon was just starting out and battling with cash flow. We had a recipe for disaster. I was only able to visit once a month, often finding that half the promised work had not been completed. I found it hard to reprimand Deon, he was a charmer and seemed genuinely grieved that he had let me down. He reminded me of John so I could forgive him almost anything. We often spoke late into the night about my search for John too, so I started to see him more as a friend than an employee.

The house was almost finished when Deon disappeared, vanishing with the last of the money from the building society, leaving me with hardly any cash to complete the building and with the unenviable task of finding another builder to finish off the job. What was it about me, was I just too trusting? I asked myself. Why did I have men walking out on me the whole time?

On top of this my sister, Kathryn, was due to arrive for the Easter holidays. Now we had no electricity, and were going to have to camp out in the house. She took it all remarkably well and survived cold showers and cooking on a gas stove. I used to take my iron with me to the local gym and surreptitiously iron my clothes in the changing room. I had definitely learned my lesson now and would be more careful with the next builder I decided to hire.

In August of that year the house was finished. I arranged to take some time off to fix it up and could finally say that it was the way I wanted it to be. It would always be badly finished as I had done so much of it on the cheap, but to me it had a certain charm. It gave me a real sense of achievement. It was mine, designed by me and paid for by me. It was, in my mind, a symbol of me reclaiming my life and the start of new beginnings.

Nigel's revelations

Life was starting to get on an even keel. I had a new job, Grotto Bay and a bit more money. It was hard to believe that this had all happened in the three years since John had left. It was my pampering Saturday when I started off with a facial and then went through to the hairdresser. I loved the hustle and bustle of the busy salon in Dunkeld on a Saturday morning. Getting there was always a bit of a mission, the traffic on Jan Smuts Avenue was snarled up at every intersection, taxi drivers weaving in and out of their lanes, furiously trying to make up time and pick up every possible passenger.

I pulled slowly into the parking area of the Dunkeld West shopping centre. I was aware that I had to be ready to counter any weird and wonderful parking manoeuvre imaginable, nothing was unexpected. And yes, true to form, a blue-rinsed lady driving a massive Mercedes reversed, without warning and without looking, right into my path. Despite the look of righteous indignation on her face, I was so bold as to flash my lights at her, being very much in her line of fire. I eased into the parking bay, which she had just vacated, and walked past the vegetable shop, then the fishmonger, carefully avoiding the bakery with its wondrous array of freshly baked bread and croissants, the smell of baking mingling with the aroma of coffee. I can't afford to get sidetracked, I kept telling myself as I walked into the salon.

I opened the door, Cindy greeted me immediately.

'Great to see you, have a seat, we are running a bit late.'

Her business partner, Ellie, greeted me from the back of the salon, a broad smile on her face. She looked so happy since her wedding a few months previously. It was warm in the salon, too warm to be wearing a jacket, so I hung it up on the coat rack. I sat leafing through an old edition of 'Hello'. It's always great to catch up on trashy reading, I thought as I prepared to ease myself into a morning of relaxation. Music played in the background, not too loudly thank goodness, as the aim of going to the hairdresser was surely to unwind and relax and not to be assailed by loud versions of rap. I breathed in the sweet smell of shampoo mixed with the harsh odour of peroxide. The stylists were chatting away happily with their customers. It was like a family here, members visiting every six weeks or so and catching up on what was happening in everyone's life.

I was summoned to the basin and let myself relax as my hair was washed and conditioned. Such a wonderful way to spend a Saturday morning, I said to myself as I eased into the pampering process. All too soon it was over and I was bundled off to a chair in front of a very unforgiving mirror. It was now Cindy's turn to transform this wet straggly hair into something resembling normality.

We compared notes of what had been happening in our lives over the last few weeks. Cindy had a young child, so was being kept very busy looking after him when she wasn't working. She was also renovating her house at the time so we swapped building horror stories.

'Ellie's looking great,' I remarked.

'She's pregnant,' Cindy replied.

'So that's why she's looking so happy.'

'Still no news of John?' Cindy asked.

I admitted that I was still reaching dead ends and there seemed to be no chance of ever finding him. He had been gone for over two years now, so long I couldn't keep up the pretence that he was coming back.

Even now I found that having people know my story was quite uncomfortable and intrusive. I didn't want them to think of me as the poor deserted wife, which was the inevitable reaction my story seemed to evoke.

'What are you going to do now?' Cindy continued. 'You can't hang about waiting forever.' She put into words what I had been thinking but was not yet ready to confront.

'I know I can't,' I answered. 'But it's not that simple. I am Catholic so there isn't much I can do about it.'

'Nonsense,' she said. 'Ellie is Italian and Catholic and was married before. Maybe you should talk to her about what she did.'

'It's not easy; it's a real mission. I'm not even sure if I would qualify,' I countered.

Cindy refused to be fobbed off, 'I'll ask Ellie to talk to you about it later.' She would not take no for an answer.

Thankfully, she then got back to the business of cutting and styling my hair, but while one of the assistants was busy blow-drying it I could see her quickly taking Ellie to one side, and having an animated conversation while glancing meaningfully in my direction.

I braced myself for Ellie's arrival and there she was, bounding up next to me, full of life and energy. She gestured that we should be left alone and sat next to me, holding my hand and said: 'You are too special to live your life alone. There is a solution. This is what I did and look how happy I am now.'

She painstakingly described her previous failed marriage and the process of obtaining an annulment. It was tough, she admitted, but at the same time it gave her a chance to start afresh. She had decided to follow this route after she had separated from her husband and had met her future husband.

'Think about it seriously,' she advised. 'I'll do anything to help, or if you need any more information, just give me a call.'

I smiled gratefully. She had given me plenty of food for thought, but it still scared me. It was such a big step and, not only that, it signalled my acceptance that my marriage was over.

I stood at the counter, paid my bill and waved a cheerful goodbye to Cindy and Ellie. I ran the gauntlet of the bakery, again refusing to be tempted into buying a calorie-laden pastry, got into my car, put the key into the ignition and then said quietly to myself, 'Maybe she has a point. I have spent years looking for John, who knows if I will ever find him. Meanwhile my life is on hold and I'm wasting so many good years.'

After my search via Interpol had yielded no conclusive results, I got in touch with a firm of private investigators in March 1995, believing that if Interpol had managed to make contact with John it should be easy to find him. I had no idea who to use and ended up hiring a firm I found through the yellow pages. I gave them all the details, parted with an up front search fee and waited. Two months went by and they confirmed that they had found no trace. I was back to square one again.

My new boss at Gilbeys, James McLachlan, knew my story and that I was still refusing to acknowledge that John was unlikely to return. One day he took me to one side, saying: 'I think you need to face the fact that John is probably not coming back.'

'I know, it's been so long, three years now but I can't give up until I find him and talk to him.'

'What have you done to try to find him?'

I explained to him I had used Interpol and a firm of private investigators with no success.

'I have used some investigators previously, let me phone them and see if they can help; they're based in Midrand quite close to the offices. They have a global network which should help.'

I smiled, 'That would be great, I don't want to give up just yet.'

He phoned them the next day and their Operations Director agreed to meet with me. At our meeting he was at pains to say that they usually only got involved in commercial matters but would handle this domestic matter as a favour, because of our business connection with them. Before doing anything they probed to see if I had any sinister motives for trying to trace John, wishing to harm him in any way, physically or financially. I assured them that this was definitely not the case.

It was a pleasure to deal with professionals. The firm of investigators I had previously engaged now seemed amateur in comparison. The new firm put one of their investigators on the case and pledged to keep their costs to a minimum as I had explained I was slowly extricating myself from the burden of debt which John had left me with.

They did not come up with any leads either, so Ellie's conversation still resonated with me. John could be dead, God forbid, and I wouldn't even know. I was living the life of a married woman, not willing to go out with anyone or enter into any new relationships. Maybe I need to face up to the fact that my marriage is over and move on; it is scary, I thought, but maybe it is the right thing to do. Even if I find John, so much has happened, the trust is no longer there. Could we rekindle our marriage? I doubt it. I sat in the car outside the hairdresser as this realisation sank in. I thought back to what Nigel had told me a few months previously. I had tried to keep it out of my mind, but the time had come to face up to reality.

'Nigel is here to see you,' Joey, my secretary said, showing him into my office.

Nigel and Anne had a hardware shop just around the corner from where I worked in Braamfontein. They had been together two years now. Nigel popped into the office to see me from time to time; we had coffee together and caught up with the latest news. It was good to know that he was close. Although he spent most of his time with Anne now, I knew I could count on him to be there for me and he made a point of oh so casually checking I was all right. He had been a constant help fixing up the house in Regent's Park, which was a bit of an uphill battle as funds were so limited. He worked hard at doing as much as he could without calling in outside help.

'Is everything all right?' I could tell there was something wrong. Nigel looked stressed and uneasy as he played with some papers on my desk. He glanced around at the pictures on my office walls, doing everything he could to avoid looking directly at me.

'What is it?' I said sharply. I needed to know whatever was bugging him.

'There's something I need to tell you,' he said.

I felt my mouth go dry. What could it be now? My life had started to reach some form of normality. Emotionally, I felt far more stable, but it still wouldn't take much to get me off balance.

I looked straight at him, 'Tell me for goodness sake.'

Joey arrived with the usual tray of coffee and biscuits. 'Sorry to interrupt,' she flushed bright red, as neither of us could help glaring at her in irritation. This was not a good moment to be interrupted. She hurried back outside to her desk muttering,' I won't disturb you again, I'll take messages.'

Nigel started again:

'Anne and I have been talking about this and she says I must tell you. I haven't wanted to because I promised John, but she has convinced me that I have to tell you now. You can't keep going on like this. I know how hard it has been for you and it's not fair for me to keep it from you any longer. I promised John and I wanted to keep my promise to him, but it has been almost two years now and I know what you have been going through. I can't be loyal to him and watch you battle so. It's killing me to keep his secret.'

My hand shook as, putting the cup back on the table, I took care not to spill the coffee. I looked at Nigel, he was agitated, nervous. I knew how much he would be battling to betray John's confidence, but I knew he equally couldn't keep me in the dark for much longer.

'Go on,' I said quietly to him, not wanting him to change his mind now. 'Please just tell me.'

'You know John didn't want you to go to the airport with him and I drove him there.'

'Yes, I know. He said he didn't want to see me sad as I waved him off, he preferred to see my smiling face when he returned.'

'I remember,' Nigel replied. He stumbled as he tried to find a way to get the words out. 'He didn't go alone.' At last managing to look me in the eye, he said, 'He was travelling with an Australian girl.'

He watched my reaction, the hurt and betrayal so clear in my eyes as they filled with tears. Yet another female in the equation, now it was a double betrayal. I swallowed and said quietly, 'Tell me, tell me everything.'

'I'm so sorry, Mary, I promised him. He was going to come back, and I didn't know what to do. As time went on I realised he was maybe never coming back and then I didn't know how to tell you. I knew it would break your heart, yet how could I tell you after all this time? Now I know you have to know, you can't keep waiting forever.'

'It's ok,' I said. I knew what it was costing Nigel to do this and I loved him for it.

'Tell me more,' I said, reaching for his hand. 'I'll be all right, I just need to know everything.'

The words came tumbling out.

'John met her in Richard's Bay; she was an Australian friend of Gary's who worked for John. She had come to see Gary for a visit and she and John became friendly, even though John was involved with Tracey there. She invited him over to Australia for a visit. I don't know if she knew he was married; she knew about Tracey but I don't think she knew about you. She's nothing like you; I don't understand why he did it. He planned to go over for a few months, get it out of his system and come back. He should have, and then everything would have been ok.'

I could see how angry he was with John and how torn he was by the loyalty he had to both of us. This was an impossible situation for him.

'What's she like?' I said shakily.

'She's not you, she could never be you,' he said gently as he got up and hugged me. 'I'm so sorry, I'm so sorry,' he kept hugging me as tears streamed down my face. 'I wish John was here then I could flatten him for what he has done to you. You didn't deserve this, you really didn't.'

'I know,' I replied, 'it's so unfair. It's sick, where does he get off playing around with people's emotions like this and then running away? What have I ever done to him to make him treat me like this? All he had to do was have the guts to tell me when he decided not to come back, is that too much to ask? He must have known what I would be going through. I don't deserve this.'

'I know, I know,' Nigel said, comforting me as he would a child. 'Anne convinced me I had to tell you. I couldn't let you go on like this, you needed to know. Keeping it from you has been tearing me apart for all these months.'

'You did the right thing. I'm upset now, but at least I know what I am dealing with. I just need to take it all in and work out what to do now.'

'Will you be all right?' he asked, glancing at his watch. 'I need to get back to the shop.'

'I'll be fine, I'll go to the Ladies, splash some water on my face and then I'll go for a walk, I need to walk. It'll calm me and then I can think. I'll be at the farm this weekend, I'm going on my own, I'll sit on the rock and think about it all.'

He gave me one last hug and headed out of the office, his step lighter now that he had rid himself of the burden of John's secret. I dabbed at my eyes, brushed my hair, and put on some lipstick as I left the office, telling Joey I was going out for a while.

My heart was racing, my mouth was dry, it was just too much to take in. A visit to my rock at the edge of the farm was definitely what I needed, my thinking rock. I sat there for hours at a time gazing at the Magaliesburg Mountains, trying to make sense of what was happening in my life. There I laughed and cried. I debated aloud with myself but always left calm and determined, having made my decisions. Nigel's revelations needed to be absorbed and then I needed to decide what I was going to do next. What kind of fool was I to be paying John's bills so that he could live the high life in Australia with yet another woman? What kind of a man was he to use me like this? Maybe this was the push I needed to take charge of my life again and stop being the helpless victim? I couldn't continue to be a doormat. I knew my friend Joan had often said that she had never known anyone love someone the way I loved John. Now even I had reached my limit.

Mother's death

The conversation with Ellie at the hairdresser played over and over in my mind. The chaos of the parking area outside didn't touch me. I was caught up in my own world with the dawning of a decision. The man in the BMW parked next to me looked at me quizzically, I was talking to myself, debating which course of action to take. My lips moved furiously as my inner debate became heated. Nigel's revelations and now the conversation with Ellie were bringing me closer to a decision.

This was not a decision to be made in haste but the thought stayed with me on and off for the next few weeks. I was worried about going through the annulment process with no guarantee of success. I wished Mother and Fred (my pet name for my father) were alive, I really needed their advice, but they weren't here and the decision would be mine and mine alone. My father had died in 1984 and my mother in 1988, several years ago already. Now as I thought back to my mother's death it brought back bitter memories of another time when John had not been there for me.

It was a balmy spring evening in 1988 when the phone rang, interrupting me as I watered the garden. I ran into the house, irritated at having to stop what I was doing.

'Hello,' Kathryn said.

It was early for her to phone as she generally only phoned in the evening when it was cheaper.

'I've just had a call from the hospital in Cambridge. They said I must drive through there now, it is looking very bad. Mother probably won't last the night.

I swallowed hard, fighting back the urge to cry. I needed to be strong for Kathryn.

'Are you driving there on your own?' I asked.

'Yes,' she said. 'Marian will join me later.'

'Are you sure you can drive?'

'Of course, don't worry, it will be fine. I'll phone you when I have news.'

'Drive safely.'

I didn't know what else to say. I put the phone down and wandered back to the garden to turn off the hosepipe. I started to pace up and down. I was so far away here in South Africa, and there was nothing I could do to help. I just had to wait and hope Mother was as comfortable as possible.

I needed John to come home; the warmth of his touch and the feeling of security he always gave me was just what I needed. He would help me get through this. I suddenly remembered that he had planned a function for some of his clients that evening and he and Nigel, who was staying with us, would have to be there as John was the host. It was such bad timing, but there wasn't much he would be able to do at this late stage. Cancelling would just not be an option. I knew that, but in my heart I hoped he could make a plan. I went into the kitchen and poured myself an orange juice. You'll get through this, I kept repeating to myself.

I heard John's key in the door, the grin on his face soon faded as he saw the grim set of my face.

'What's wrong, sweetheart?' he said, reaching for my hand.

'Kathryn's just phoned,' I explained. 'She has to go to Cambridge, it is looking very bad.'

He hugged me tight. 'Don't worry, I'm here. I'll look after you.'

I felt myself relax as he held me. I knew it wasn't going to be all right but I could pretend for now.

He waited for me to stop sobbing and looked at me apologetically. 'You know I have the party tonight don't you? It's with some really important customers, I can't cancel now, and their contracts are worth a lot of money. You do understand don't you? I'll come back as soon as I can. I hate the thought of you being alone.'

He went out to the flat at the back to tell Nigel what had happened and to make arrangements for their night out.

I tried to stay composed, getting upset wasn't helping anybody, and my sadness was starting to mingle with anger at John's focus on business. I needed him tonight far more than his business acquaintances did. Could he not just for once replace his ambition and hunger for money with compassion for my situation?

It seemed not. He scurried around, showering quickly and then taking an age to pick out just the right thing to wear. 'I have to look good tonight,' he said as he saw me watching him.

'I know,' I replied and turning on my heel I left the bedroom. I wanted them to go as soon as possible. If they had to go, then let them go and leave me in peace to get through the evening in my own way.

'I'll be thinking of you,' John said as he got into the car.

Nigel smiled at me, 'We'll be back as soon as we can.'

I went back into the house closing the door firmly behind me, tears streaming down my face. Was I crying for my mother or with frustration at John's insensitivity? I didn't know, but gave in to my emotions. I cried for almost an hour, letting out all my heartache until calm descended. Now I just had to wait.

My mother had been to visit us for three months at the beginning of the year. She loved to visit South Africa during the English winter. Our house in Mondeor had a very comfortable guest cottage at the bottom of the garden. We toured around the country visiting Cape Town, the Garden Route and many other interesting sights closer to Johannesburg. She had occupied herself while we were at work with writing some of her life story in an old exercise book, calling it 'Green are the hills far away'.

Her last trip had been a little different in that Father Joe joined us for the last month. He had just retired as the principal chaplain for the RAF and was taking the opportunity to spend some time in Africa. He had been a missionary in Tanzania in his younger days but had never made it to South Africa. We had been close since my teenage years when we were based at RAF Oakington, near Cambridge. He visited my parents most Saturday evenings to watch *Match of the Day*. I enjoyed his quick wit and sense of humour. He was a small, stocky man with a broad Irish accent, very approachable, not a bit like any priest I had met before. I felt I could talk to him about anything. His constant jokes belied a really caring and good man who quietly touched the lives of many. I was hoping he would like John when he met him, as they were both such special people in my life. I needn't have been concerned, they got on like a house on fire.

As the holiday came to an end Father Joe took me to one side and said, 'I'm happy to see you so settled. Your father would have been so proud. John is a great guy and I can see how much he loves you.'

I knew Mother felt the same way. She showed me what she had written in her journal about our wedding:

> *I am so happy for her, they are so well suited and are so happy together. Kathryn has met her John, if she is as happy with him as Mary is with John, I will be content. I'm very happy to have him as a son-in-law. My only regret is that Paddy didn't have the chance to get to know him properly.*

The week before the end of the holiday my mother mentioned that she seemed to be losing weight. It seemed strange, as we had been eating out frequently and she should have been putting on weight if anything.

'It's probably the heat,' I told her, 'you're sweating it all out.'

I couldn't help feeling uneasy though. My mother and father were both heavy smokers. My father had died of lung cancer almost four years previously and I had always feared that my mother would also develop the disease.

My worst fears were realised when she was diagnosed with lung cancer a month after she arrived back in Cambridge. It was so difficult being far away when she was ill. I did manage to go over for a week two months later. It was terrible to see how she had wasted away. What could I say to her? We both knew her death was inevitable yet we talked about so many inconsequential things, avoiding the only subject that really mattered.

As I left for Heathrow and my flight back to Johannesburg, the time came to say our goodbyes at the bus station in central Cambridge. I had experienced the same painful departure from my father four years previously. I hugged her, saying goodbye, boarding the bus knowing I would never see her again. Same bus, same departure time, same friends with me. I waved to her as the bus slowly moved away, her gaunt figure lifting her hand weakly as she waved her last goodbye.

My last image of her kept running through my mind as I sat in bed that night, watching the minutes tick over on the clock radio and thinking of Kathryn and our cousin there at her bedside. It was useless trying to sleep, too many thoughts raced through my head. Reading didn't help either, I had been crying so much my eyes were puffy and swollen, too irritated to distinguish properly the words on the pages. I tossed off the floral duvet, I was hot and fidgety. I just couldn't settle. Maybe I should walk, I said to myself, that always calms me. I put on my dressing gown and went out to the garden, making sure I was close enough to the house to hear the phone. I gazed at the stars and walked around the garden once, twice, twenty times. The rhythmic pounding of my feet on the grass slowed my heartbeat and I started to feel calmer. How much longer can it be?

I prayed quietly, finding comfort in the familiarity of prayers I had said from childhood. I continued to walk. It will soon be light, where on earth can John be? I wondered. Surely the function is finished by now? The ringing of the phone interrupted my thoughts. I rushed into the house. It was my cousin Marian. 'It's over,' she said. 'It was peaceful, Kathryn was with her. Is John there with you?'

'No, not at the moment.'

'Will you be all right?'

'Of course,' I replied. 'I'll phone tomorrow and check the arrangements for the funeral.'

I replaced the receiver and collapsed in a crumpled heap on the floor, sobs wracking my body. I felt so alone. Where was John when I needed him? A feeling of nausea came over me. It had all been too much. I just couldn't cope any more. What must I do now? I told myself to take deep breaths and gathered myself up from the floor staggering to the kitchen to get some water. I forced it down, gagging at first. I felt myself become calmer. You have to get some sleep, I told myself, there is a lot to be done tomorrow. I wandered back to the bedroom, climbed back into bed, sitting up, clutching my knees and staring straight ahead, shaking uncontrollably. That was how I was when John eventually returned from his business function, at 3 am, reeking of alcohol and enveloping me in a boozy hug.

'I'm so sorry,' he kept repeating. 'I'm so sorry.

'I know,' I replied.

'Go to sleep now, I'll help you organise everything tomorrow.' He held me tight, falling into a deep sleep. I listened to his snoring as I stared into the distance.

Crisis of faith

A few weeks after my conversation with Ellie at the hairdressers, Geraldine invited me over to her house in Florida on a Saturday evening for supper. I had known Geraldine on and off for many years and had often seen her at the Irish Club while we were living in Hillbrow. She was a good friend and very aware of the John situation.

Father John Cleary was also there. It was good to see him; he was a young priest from Carlow in Ireland, living in Dobsonville in Soweto. He was tall, gangly, with thinning sandy hair and a wicked sense of humour. Geraldine had obviously primed him about the fact that I was considering an annulment. At the end of the meal he sat down next to me on the pink floral sofa next to the fireplace, his voice low and compassionate.

'Mary, me darling, I know it has been hard for you this last while, with John going away. I know you are thinking about getting an annulment,' he said.

'I am,' I replied 'but I don't know quite where to start.'

'Why don't you speak to the Bishop's office in Pretoria?' he suggested 'There is a priest there called Emil Blaser, he may be able to help you.'

He gave me the phone number. I wrote it down in my pocket diary and went to help Geraldine pack away the dishes. 'Do it!' she said. 'It will be ok, you'll see.'

I kept the phone number with me for several weeks. Speaking to someone about an annulment seemed to be admitting defeat. I toyed with making the call and one Friday afternoon, sitting at my desk, I convinced myself that I had nothing to lose. Finding out about an annulment didn't mean I had to go through with it. It would simply give me the information to make a decision.

'Hello, this is Mary Monaghan speaking; I would like to make an appointment to see Father Blaser.'

'Please hold on while I transfer you to his secretary.'

I waited for what seemed like an eternity – it had taken me two weeks to pluck up the courage to make this call. I had to be sure that I was doing the right thing.

I closed my office door so that I wouldn't be interrupted, but I could still hear the chatter of Anna and Beauty outside the door. Unconscious of the turmoil I was in, normality reigned in their world.

At long last the secretary came back, 'The earliest he can see you is on the 22nd of March at 2 p.m.'

'Thank you, that will be fine,' I responded, smiling ruefully to myself.

An appointment on John's birthday, how appropriate was that? I put the phone down and tried to slow my racing heart. I was just enquiring anyway, there was no harm in that, and one step at a time was the way to go. At the time that Father John had suggested I speak to Father Blaser it seemed like a great idea, but I wasn't so sure any more. Time would tell, and I had to wait ten days to see him.

The day of John's thirty-second birthday, 22nd March 1995, arrived and I told Anna, my secretary, that I had an appointment in Pretoria that afternoon as I shut my office door behind me, clutching the directions to the Bishop's office in Pretoria. I had dressed appropriately, at least in my eyes, for this meeting. A sensible skirt with a classic shirt and jacket, all in tones of beige and black, nothing too vibrant. I wanted them to see that I was taking this seriously.

I took a deep breath as I settled into my car; this could be the beginning of the end. I was finally admitting it could be over. Just laying out the facts to a stranger was going to be scary; thank goodness it was to a priest who was used to handling these kinds of conversations.

Come on; come on, I muttered under my breath as I realised there must be an accident up ahead; something was delaying traffic on the M1. I didn't know Pretoria very well and didn't want to arrive late. At last the traffic officer waved me past the accident scene, a red Golf and a white Corolla standing mangled in the middle lane of the highway. I'm due there in twenty minutes; hopefully I'll get there in time, I said to myself.

I managed to conquer the vagaries of Pretoria's one-way system and parked outside the building with five minutes to spare. Just enough time to dab on some lipstick, brush my hair and generally make myself presentable. I left my cell phone in the cubby-hole of the car; I couldn't be interrupted during the meeting. One last look to make sure I was respectable and then in I went to see Father Blaser.

A young receptionist lifted her head from the latest copy of the 'You' magazine and asked if she could help. 'I'm here to see Father Blaser' I said. 'I'll tell him you're here, please take a seat.'

I made a valiant attempt to pretend to read one of the magazines on the coffee table but the images were just a blur. I could feel my heart beating furiously. My cheeks were flushed, what was I doing here?

Any chance to flee went out of the window as she said, 'I'll show you to Father Blaser's office.'

She led me through the corridors painted a hospital green, sterile and gloomy, to a sparsely furnished office.

Father Blaser stood up from behind his desk. 'Please sit down,' he said. He was somehow different to what I had imagined. He was of average height, with black hair, his black trousers and shirt immaculate, set off by his crisp white dog collar. Very much a priest, but evidently a priest who cared about his appearance. He had no time for small talk: 'Why are you here?'

'I want to find out about getting an annulment.'

'Are you pregnant, about to get married? Divorced?'

'No, I thought I wasn't supposed to get divorced and that one should get an annulment before getting into any other relationships,' I said, quite startled at his approach.

He continued to spit out questions relentlessly. 'Why haven't you got a divorce? What makes you think you qualify for an annulment? What have you done to save your marriage? Why do you want an annulment now?'

Bombarded by this litany of questions, I stammered my responses, trying to explain that I didn't realise I needed to be divorced before I could apply for an annulment. I tried to explain the circumstances in which I found myself and why I thought an annulment was appropriate, stumbling over my words, sensing his hostility and impatience.

'Did your husband beat you? Did he abuse drugs?' He just kept on going, hardly allowing me time to respond, constantly on the attack.

My voice shook, but I would not leave without asking the one question which I needed answered. 'My husband has disappeared, I have spent years looking for him, and there is no telling if I will ever find him. Must I spend the rest of my life as a married woman despite the fact that I don't know if he is alive or dead and I have no control over this situation? Would I qualify for an annulment?'

'You should have got a divorce,' he said curtly 'and as for an annulment, who knows, there are no guarantees. People need to take the institution of marriage more seriously. If you want to take it further maybe the head of the Marriage Tribunal can help. His name is Father Kieran McIvor; he is based in Bryanston. I really don't know if it would be worth pursuing this, but if you really insist, maybe you should talk to him.'

'Thank you Father,' I said as I left the office, struggling to hold back the tears, trying to understand why I was being put on trial for something that I couldn't help. I made it to the car, and put my hands on the steering wheel sobbing my heart out. I was battling to reconcile the Church that I had belonged to for all these years with the Church that had just confronted me, mean, vicious and unbending.

I reached over to the glove compartment and took out my cell phone. One message – hopefully not the office, as I was really shaky now and not ready for any office issues. It was a message from the private investigator I had employed at James McLachlan's instigation. I was trying everything to find John. I had given him every last detail I could think of to help him trace John. How difficult could it be? I kept telling myself it would only be a matter of time. But I hardly expected it now.

'I have news for you,' he said.

I phoned back immediately, thinking to myself, how much more can I take today on John's birthday?

He picked up the phone immediately.

'We have traced a John Monaghan in Sydney; it may be your husband. I will have more details tomorrow. We have him under surveillance.'

I finished the call, threw the phone on the floor and started to sob. What is going on? I asked myself. Is it a sign that I shouldn't be doing this? It's just too much of a coincidence, who would believe this? Half an hour passed and I got myself sufficiently under control to drive back to Johannesburg, muttering under my breath at the treatment I had received, while at the same time imagining how I would react if I managed to make contact with John.

I now concentrated on getting information from the private investigator. He sent me the profile of the person they had found a week later, but no luck. He was the wrong age and build. Yet another dead end, and a waste of yet another Australian visa in my passport.

This was the second time I had arranged to get an Australian visa. I didn't want to find John and then wait for weeks before I could go over and see him. I wanted to be prepared to fly to Australia at short notice. I played around with various scenarios in my mind as to how I would meet him. Would I turn up on his doorstep unexpectedly? What would my opening words to him be? It kept my mind occupied but added to my stress levels and levels of anticipation. I was in a state of constant tension and anxiety, expecting to find him at any moment, whilst still reconciling myself to the fact that I should move on with my life. My friends encouraged me to stop searching and put it all behind me but I was driven to continue. I wasn't sure if it was just a matter of pride, not wanting him to get the better of me or was it simply the need to get answers to my questions? I wasn't really sure but all I knew was that I wouldn't rest until I had found John, no matter how long it took.

The next few months were a time of intense introspection. Through all the trauma of the last few years the Catholic Church had been my rock, it had grounded me. I had clung to my faith as the anchor which would hold me fast. I prayed, lit candles, and attended Mass. It gave me solace and the strength to continue through all the hardship I had endured. Now the Church as I knew it no longer existed for me. I felt betrayed, abandoned, and alone, now not just by John, but by the Church too. I could not bring myself to go back to Mass. What purpose would it serve when I had such feelings of anger mixed with sadness at the loss of something which was so dear to me?

A few months later I was back at the hairdresser. Ellie came up to me, not too closely this time, as by now she was seven months pregnant and rather rotund. 'How did it go?' she asked. ' I'm sorry I missed you last time you were here but I was off sick.'

'You're never going to believe this,' I said telling her my tale of woe.

'I can't believe it,' she said. 'Father Blaser's quite young, so you would think he would be liberal. Where does he get off, giving you such a hard time?'

I explained to her that it had triggered off a major crisis of faith for me and I was battling to reconcile what had happened with my faith in the Church.

'He's only one priest,' she said, 'why don't you speak to Father McIvor from the Marriage Tribunal? I've seen him at Mass, he's quite old, in his seventies, but seems like a really nice man. What harm can it do?'

'Not much,' I said begrudgingly, 'maybe I will.' Again I hesitated; did I really want to put myself through this again?

Several months passed and then one day I decided why not? What is the worst that can happen? He can just be beastly to you that's all, at least now you know what to expect. I closed the office door, picked up the phone, dialled and, to my surprise, got through immediately to Father McIvor. He had a soft Irish accent.

'What can I do for you, my dear?' he said gently.

I explained that I wanted to get an annulment and repeated the conversation I had had with Father Blaser.

'Please tell me your story, take your time, there's no rush,' he said, his gentle tones giving me the confidence to give the full story.

I recounted John's disappearance and my search for him. As I was telling my story he led me on with murmurs of encouragement and interest. I explained why I felt I needed to close this chapter of my life and move on.

'You have been through a very difficult time, my dear,' he said softly.

'I know, I just want to find out if I could be granted an annulment.'

'There are no guarantees,' he said 'but let me put it to you like this, if you were my niece I would encourage you to go ahead.'

I took a deep breath, he had listened to me and it seemed like there was a chance.

'What must I do?' I asked.

'This may sound strange,' he said 'but you need to be divorced first. We are not legally able to look at annulling a marriage until a divorce has taken place, you may start both processes simultaneously though.'

'There are forms to be completed which I can send to your parish priest. Then we need to interview two friends of yours and two of your husband's. We will also interview you. The process will take several months. Please call me if you need help with anything. I think you are a very brave lady and I wish you everything of the best. God bless you, my dear.'

'Thank you, Father.'

I smiled to myself as I put the phone down. Now I had seen the face of the Church that I had been brought up to expect, kind, compassionate and loving.

I'm going to do this, I said to myself, as I opened the office door, determined to get the ball rolling. The despair of the previous months was forgotten as I looked at the future with renewed hope.

Annulment

'The Mass is ended, go in peace to love and serve the Lord.'

I took a deep breath and gathered up my handbag and car keys from the pew in the church in Braamfontein. I had received a call from my parish priest to say that he had received the annulment forms. All that remained was to collect them from the sacristy after Mass and set the process in motion. All so simple, but so final.

The priest was outside in the church grounds, greeting his parishioners. He probably knew me by sight but wouldn't know my name, as I liked to retain my anonymity when I worshipped. What did it matter who I was or what story I had to tell? It was a bright, sunny winter's morning in Johannesburg, in June 1996, the kind of day when you count your blessings and revel in the joy of just being alive. I stood on one side, waiting. At last he was on his own. I went up to him and asked about the forms. He smiled gently at me.

'Come with me my dear, I have them in the sacristy for you.' We walked together into the room where he made his preparations to say Mass. His desk was a jumble of papers. He scrabbled around and eventually found what he was looking for and handed the brown envelope to me. 'Please let me know if there is anything I can do to help, or if you have any questions.'

I nodded quickly. I just wanted to get out of there and find out what I needed to do. Now he knew who I was and some of my story, it made me uncomfortable.

It had been over three years since John had gone away and I had at last come to terms with the fact that he was not coming back. I had kicked against getting a divorce, believing that was not the correct thing to do, but after Father McIvor had explained to me that a divorce was necessary to apply for an annulment through the Catholic Church I realised that I had no option. I had been brought up to believe that marriage was forever and that divorce was not possible. I believed that a couple should work to overcome their problems and that divorce was an admission of failure. Through my conversation with Father McIvor I realised that it wasn't as simple as that. If only Father Blaser had explained the matter to me properly over a year ago I could have already started to move on.

As with most things during this period the divorce was not so straightforward. Lynn's new husband, Paul, was a lawyer and he referred me to a firm of attorneys based in Sandton. There was a complication in that I had no address for John and that meant that a summons could not be served on him. Advertisements had to be drawn up and placed in Australian newspapers advising him that I was seeking a divorce. This all came at a cost. The female lawyer who was handling my case was very sympathetic and helped to keep costs to the minimum, but due to the complexity of my situation it wasn't that easy. I tightened my belt once more and managed to scrape together the money to cover the costs.

Finally, the court date arrived almost a year later, March 1997. I had given the attorney copies of reports from the private investigators I had engaged in 1995 and 1996, and also a card from John's mother asking me to let her know if I heard from him, all to support my statement that I didn't know his whereabouts.

It was a crisp autumn day when I made my appearance in court, accompanied by a junior attorney. I sat on a cold bench watching sadly as marriages were dissolved, feeling the emotions of the people taking the witness stand to tell their stories. Several of my friends had offered to come with me but I wanted to do this on my own. I felt calm and composed; it was almost surreal, divorce was meaningless to me, nor did I recognise it as a process. To me it was a necessary step on the way to annulment. But I won't feel any less married after today, I thought.

At long last they called my name, I took the stand and my attorney asked me some questions to confirm the facts of my case. The judge looked at me compassionately. She had given some of the other people quite a hard time, but not me. 'It must have been difficult for you,' she said; 'I wish you luck in the future.'

She granted the divorce and awarded costs against John. A token gesture, since he was not around to settle them. I left the courthouse, got in my car and headed back to the office, it was just another day.

I was able to prepare for the annulment while the divorce was in process. The annulment questionnaire was long and probing, taking me back to my childhood, asking questions about my early life and then leading up to my single years and my marriage to John. I decided to fill it in one Sunday when I had plenty of time and when I knew I would have no interruptions. It was going to be difficult, as I had to revisit all the aspects of my marriage and think about things I had spent the last few years trying to forget. I was determined to be honest; it was pointless trying to write what the tribunal wanted to hear, adjusting my story to gain advantage. I was going to tell it like it was and hopefully it would be sufficient for them to grant me an annulment.

I looked at the sections it covered. It was very comprehensive:

My family background and upbringing
My relationships with my parents and brothers/sisters
Any problems in the home
The way I acquired knowledge about sex and marriage
My relationships with any men other than my husband
My husband's background

How we came to know each other
Our courtship
Circumstances leading to the wedding
Length of married life and any problems experienced
Reasons for the breakdown of the marriage
Current status

I sat quietly in the lounge, soft music playing in the background and settled down to write. I stroked the Cong Love Token which John had given me so long ago and which always sat on the coffee table.

It is a symbol of love, always watching ever giving, whoever carries it has a promise of love in their arms.

I knew this was going to be an emotional day. I had photocopied the form, my handwriting is large and expressive and I didn't want to run out of space. It was just as well I had done so, as I found the pages filling quickly with the story of my life. I was still loyal to John and was anxious that they didn't see him in too bad a light. I was at pains to explain that although I didn't know the reasons for his disappearance, he had generally been a good and loving husband to me. Maybe this wouldn't help my case but it was the truth and I needed them to know that I had now forgiven him for what he had done. I had battled to accept the unfairness of what he had done to me, understanding why he had decided not to return to South Africa to face his responsibilities, but angry with him for not having the courage to let me know that he wasn't coming back.

'A postcard would have done, without a return address just to let me know he wasn't planning on coming back,' I had said to Pam just the weekend before as we sat on the stoep at the farm, watching the sun go down and talking about the annulment process. 'I would have been upset but at least I could have gone on with my life. I've wasted four good years now, in limbo, just waiting. If only he had had the guts to tell me what was going on.'

She reached for my hand. 'You're right; you must take control of your life. Accept what has happened and start living for yourself again.' Her words made sense to me. What John had done to me was cruel and spineless but I did not want to come out of the experience bitter and twisted. I felt saddened and hurt that someone whom I had loved so much could treat me so badly.

I continued with the questionnaire. My hand was getting tired, I wasn't used to writing so much at a stretch, but the annulment questions were plentiful and needed comprehensive answers. I finished the details of our courtship and the build up to our wedding, so many memories were running through my mind. I took a break and walked in the garden, trying to relax and deal with the emotions that surfaced. I needed to compose myself again, before completing the story of the rest of our life together.

As evening approached I finished the questionnaire. Now all that remained was to take a copy for my records and post the original to the tribunal. They would then advise me of a date when I would be called for an interview to discuss the details of my marriage and make recommendations on the merits of my case. They would also need to interview some of our friends to get an outsider's view of our marriage. I knew it was a difficult thing to ask any of my friends to do but it had to be done. Ideally, at least one of them had to be a friend of John's to keep the balance right. I needed friends who had been close to us for several years. I thought of Lynn, Wendy and Nigel. I wasn't sure if they would do it, it wouldn't be easy for them to talk about our marriage to a total stranger, but they all willingly agreed.

The tricky thing was that only Nigel knew the full story about John's other relationships. The only deception the other friends knew about was his fictitious journey to Mozambique. I hadn't been able to bring myself to tell any of my friends about the women in his life, maybe I still didn't fully accept the reality of what he had done. I explained this in the questionnaire:

> *I only found out after John left that, in addition to being married to me, and living with someone else, he actually went to Australia with yet another woman.*

I still wanted to maintain this confidentiality and continued:

> *I have always been very private about my personal life and felt I did not want my friends to know about his infidelity as I did not want them to judge him especially if we were trying to become reconciled. In view of this I would request*

that you do not reveal this to Lynn and Wendy when you interview them. I still love my husband and feel a loyalty to him and, despite everything, I do not want them to think badly of him.

I posted the forms to the marriage tribunal and waited. Several months passed and then a call came through from the secretary of the tribunal. 'I'm afraid there is quite a backlog of cases, so if you want to be interviewed by a priest, it will take a few months still. If you are prepared to be interviewed by a lay person, we can fit you in quite soon.'

I was more than happy to be interviewed by a lay person, especially as it was a woman, Brenda Farry. They gave me her phone number and asked me to phone to make arrangements. I was going to be interviewed first and then she would contact my friends individually after that.

I looked at my diary; I had nothing much on for the next few days so hopefully she would be able to see me soon. I just wanted to get it over and done with. I phoned her number wondering what kind of a person she would be, visualising a staid old granny type. Instead a vibrant woman answered the phone. I explained who I was and she arranged to see me the next evening. She gave me directions to her home in Craighall Park and said she was looking forward to meeting me. She sounded warm and friendly and told me not to worry, it would be a relaxed chat; I just needed to be myself.

I phoned my friends to tell them that the moment had finally arrived. They were positive and supportive, but I could tell they were also concerned. They knew how big this was for me and how much I had set my heart on an annulment, but they were worried at me having to go through the trauma of an interview where I relived the past. I made light of it and played down the whole thing, but deep down I was afraid and stressed.

What if they don't see things the way I do? What if they don't think I have sufficient grounds? What if this whole intrusive process is for nothing? I forced these niggling doubts out of my mind and prepared for the interview by re-reading my copy of the questionnaire. If the truth wasn't going to help, then so be it. It was all I had.

I left the office in Midrand and drove through to Craighall Park.

My appointment was for 5.30 p.m. and I had left plenty of time to battle through the traffic. As ever, I hated the thought of being late. I arrived five minutes early, parked my car in the large driveway and walked towards the front door. Brenda lived in a beautiful old house with a garden bursting with colour. I could hear the sound of a fountain in the distance. It seemed like a happy, friendly place.

She opened the door, a wide smile on her face. 'Please come in, we'll sit in the lounge; it will be quiet there. I've been so looking forward to meeting you since I read your story. You seem so positive and forgiving and still so full of love. I found your story very touching.'

She bustled around in the kitchen making us coffee and then sat down next to me and explained how the interview would work. She led me through some of the questions I had already answered, probing and clarifying where necessary. It was just like speaking to a friend, easy and informal. She had tissues handy for the difficult moments and gave me time to take her through the intimate details of my relationship with John. The two hours I was with her flew by. Eventually it was over, I felt drained and shaky, but happy that I had been given the opportunity to tell my story, personally.

She walked me to my car. 'Thank you for coming,' she said. 'You are a very special person. I'm sure everything will be all right.'

I got into my car and headed back into town, tearful but relieved. Finally I accepted it was the beginning of the end.

'Did you ever do drugs?' Wendy asked when she phoned me the following week.

'Why do you ask?' I said.

'They asked me that in the interview and I didn't know what to say.'

She had been the first to be interviewed, followed by Lynn and Nigel.

'What should we say?' they all asked before being interviewed, worried that they might say something which could be detrimental to my case.

'Just tell the truth,' I told all of them. What will be will be.'

I had been told that the outcome might still be a few months away, so I settled into my routine again, putting all thoughts of the annulment out of my head. I was busy at work, preparing for a management team-building weekend in the Drakensberg. I felt strong, I had taken action, I was proud that on my birthday that year I beat the temptation to play the answering-machine tape. I was not going to listen to John's voice; I had to move on.

Our office weekend away was upon us. It was now the last weekend in May. We were travelling to the mountains in two cars and had booked two self-catering cottages. We were going to hike, cook and play charades around the fire. It promised to be a relaxing weekend. I wandered around the office, talking to the staff about our trip. It was autumn and the weather was still good, most of us had plans for outdoor activities before the onset of winter.

'I have a message for you,' Anna said as I walked back into my office. She handed it to me. 'Please phone Sister Rita,' it read.

I'd been for some blood tests a few days before. What could it mean? I felt perfectly well.

I dialled the number and took a few seconds to realise that Sister Rita was not a nursing sister, but an Irish nun calling from the Marriage Tribunal. 'Congratulations, your annulment is through. I'm so happy for you. We'll be sending the paperwork through to you. Congratulations, my dear.'

'Thank you,' I replied battling to reconcile her cheery, excited voice with the emptiness inside me. Tears streamed down my face. It was over. My marriage was over. John was never coming back into my life. For the first time I acknowledged that I was truly alone. I needed time to myself to work through my emotions but it wasn't to be.

A few minutes later Wayne was dialling my extension, 'We're ready to go. All the cars are packed.'

'Just give me a few minutes,' I said, trying to compose myself before walking out to join them.

Gorilla trekking

'How do you fancy going to trek for gorillas?' Peter said to me over a cup of coffee at the Brazilian Coffee shop in Sun City.

I looked at him over the newspaper, 'What do you mean?'

'Why don't we find out about the trips they do to Uganda, gorilla trekking, it might be quite an adventure?'

I didn't know what to say, it was such an unexpected idea. Maybe something so out of the ordinary might just be what I needed. 'What made you think of that?' I asked.

Peter responded that a friend of his had done the trip a few years previously and highly recommended it. The gorillas were endangered and with the continuous poaching in the area it was unlikely that they would survive much longer.

I grinned at him, 'Why not? Let's look into it on Monday.'

Maybe this was just what I needed to take me out of myself. When my annulment had been granted two months previously, I started to accept that this was the end of my marriage. I was not going to find John and had to start thinking about moving on. I spent the next few months in a spiral of depression, isolating myself from my friends, refusing to go out. It was a renewed period of mourning for what I had lost. I had finally admitted defeat and acknowledged that John was out of my life forever. Although I had come to terms intellectually with it, emotionally I was very raw. It felt like an admission of failure, I had had no control over what had happened to me and was powerless in terms of fixing it. I was unable to save my marriage; I had been helpless and disempowered throughout the whole process. I needed in some way to acknowledge that I had, to an extent, regained some control. After all, I had made the decision to go through the divorce and the annulment process, I had opened myself to new possibilities and, although in my heart I wasn't quite ready to fully accept everything, I could start to act more independently. A trip to the gorillas could be just the thing.

I remembered how I had met Peter through Wendy just after Steve had been killed. Both she and I shunned contact with the Irish crowd we used to see regularly, it was just too painful, too many memories. In addition, I found it difficult to handle all the questions they inevitably asked. Have you heard from John? Where is he? When is he coming back? We had become very close. Wendy often remarked that, in some ways, it was easier for her, she knew what had happened to Steve. She wasn't plagued by uncertainty as I was, she knew what she was dealing with.

We were sitting outside one warm summer's evening in 1996 when I told her of an invitation I had received to a reception being held for Mary Robinson who, at the time, was the President of Ireland. The invitation was addressed to Mary Monaghan and guest; it was now common knowledge within our Irish community that John was nowhere to be found. The reception was a cocktail affair to be held at the Carlton Hotel in Johannesburg on the 28th March. I loved these kinds of functions; they were a chance to dress up and mingle with interesting people, but there was the problem of the 'guest'. It was becoming increasingly difficult for me to attend functions on my own and, although I knew that I could quite easily do so, I didn't want to endure the pitying stares of the other guests. The Irish community was a close knit one and my situation was definitely a scandal in their eyes. On the other hand, I so wanted to attend the function. I was starting to question my decision to avoid contact with the community, why should I keep running away? I had done nothing wrong.

'Why don't you ask Peter?' Wendy asked. 'He's good company, young and attractive, that will give them something to talk about.'

I looked at her, horrified. 'Peter wouldn't want to go there with me, he's so much younger and would probably find it incredibly boring.'

'Nonsense,' she replied, 'he loves things like this and he enjoys your company. I'll ask him.'

I would have been embarrassed to ask him myself, but was secretly glad that Wendy was prepared to ask on my behalf. It would be great to go with Peter, not to mention the satisfaction of giving people something other than John to gossip about.

The next day Wendy phoned, 'It's all fixed up, Peter will pick you up at 5.30 p.m. and you can go through together.' I thanked her profusely; it would be great to go with someone. I was sick of feeling like a spare part at parties.

I left work early on the day of the reception, giving myself enough time to shower and change. I wanted to look my best, the last thing I wanted to do was look stressed and haggard. I chose the inevitable black outfit, a skirt and a black top; black high heels and glossy black tights completed the outfit. I looked sexy but classy. I applied discreet makeup, brushed my hair, applied one last coat of lipstick and was ready to face the world. Just as I took one last look in the mirror Peter arrived, looking oh so smart in a navy blazer and chinos. I grinned to myself, I knew arriving with him was going to cause a stir but why not? It would be fun to cause a bit of havoc.

It was a short drive to the Carlton; although the sky was threatening there was no sign of the Highveld afternoon thundershowers which were almost inevitable at this time of the year. We were driving against the traffic so we made it through to the hotel in good time and parked underground so it wouldn't be a problem if it rained.

Peter held the car door open for me. 'You look very nice,' he said as I straightened my skirt and made my way to the lift.

I couldn't help but feel nervous, it had been so long since I had faced so many of my Irish acquaintances in one room. It was going to be nerve-wracking and I didn't want to get upset. Having Peter with me would be such help, but, all the same, it wasn't going to be easy.

The lift opened at the floor where the reception was being held. We walked straight to the registration counter to give our names. Happily, I didn't recognise the faces of the people manning the counter. Then we headed for the bar, a little Dutch courage to help things along. I scanned the room for familiar faces and spotted some people I knew. Peter and I were sipping our drinks, preparing to mingle when Joan came up to us. It was great to see a familiar face. She also knew Peter well as she too was a friend of Wendy's.

'I'm so glad you decided to come,' she said. 'You've been avoiding everyone for so long. It's great Peter is with you, that will give them something to talk about.' And it did. I watched people recognise me from across the room, make their way towards me, see Peter, do a dou-ble take and generally beat a hasty retreat. I was enjoying this; we were having such fun, spending time with some of my friends. Those that knew me well enough were not taken aback by Peter's presence.

It was a great evening and the start of a wonderful friendship with Peter. We became close friends, frequently going out together. He be-came my companion for most of the functions to which I was invited. He shared my love of food and wine, coupled with a sense of adventure and spontaneity to which I could relate. So when he broached the subject of the gorillas with me in those desolate months after the an-nulment I was happy to plan a trip with him. I was confident that we would be good travelling companions. Both of us had a great desire to travel more in Africa. We didn't understand too much what a visit to the gorillas would entail, but it sounded exotic and exciting so what more could we want?

Neither of us knew who we should contact, so we set about finding out when we got back to work after our Sun City trip. We knew it was a specialised holiday and that we couldn't do it on our own, but that was the extent of our knowledge. After several failed attempts to source a tour operator, we managed to find a group called Wild Frontiers who operated such trips. They faxed me through the information. As soon as I received it I phoned Peter excitedly; 'It looks amazing; I think we should meet to go through all the details.'

We arranged to meet the next evening at Hyde Park for dinner. The itinerary looked great, one drawback being that most of the time was spent in tents and neither of us was an experienced camper. We devoured the information over a couple of glasses of wine.

'Don't worry about the camping,' Peter said. 'Look here, it says we may be asked to assist with erecting the tents but only if they are running late, so it will be fine.'

Hiking into the mountains to track the gorillas sounded quite strenuous but we resolved to make sure that we increased our levels of fitness to cope with it. By the end of the evening we were sure that we wanted to do the trip. I would make contact with the tour operator the next day and start looking at possible dates. I felt so excited. I knew this was just what the doctor had ordered. It was quite pricey but worth it. It would be the trip of a lifetime. How many people could say they had seen the gorillas in their natural habitat? We settled on a date in May, just two months later. Both of us liked to do things on the spur of the moment; neither of us was very good at planning things too far in advance.

In the next few days, we received the list of things to pack. We couldn't carry too much as we were travelling in a group of eight in an overland truck. Many nights were spent planning what we would take, Peter insisting that, no matter what, he would take sufficient titbits to snack on, there was no way he was going hungry. My sister Kathryn sent me the video of *Gorillas in the Mist* from London to help with preparations and to show us a bit of what we could expect. Our excitement was becoming palpable; we just knew that this was going to be an experience we wouldn't forget in a hurry. Travelling in a group was something neither of us enjoyed, we cherished our independence, but we accepted that this was a trip we couldn't do on our own. Travelling in this area was dangerous. Civil war had just broken out in the Democratic Republic of Congo, and Rwanda was still reeling from years of ethnic violence.

The morning of our departure, Peter's sister, Dimi, dropped us off at the airport in Johannesburg; we carried our rucksacks into the terminal, both laden with snacks and the maximum allowance of wine. We were taking no chances on suffering from either hunger or thirst. We looked for the Uganda Airways counter, a flight to Entebbe on Uganda Airways, even that had an intrepid ring to it!

We checked in our luggage, went through passport control, visited the duty-free shop and then sat on one of the benches, eyeing-up the people passing by and trying to figure out who might be in our group. Could it be that older lady with what looks to be her daughter? Or maybe those other two men dressed in khaki and wearing hiking boots? We laughed and joked about the unending possibilities. At long last they called the flight. The adventure was about to begin. We settled back, it wasn't a long flight and we would see some interesting scenery. We were going to be met at the airport and only then would we be certain who was on the trip with us.

We circled Entebbe airport and landed on a runway adjoining the one on which languished the burnt out remains of the aircraft hijacked all those years ago, which featured in the film *Raid on Entebbe*. The aircraft doors opened and the humidity and smells of Africa penetrated the cabin. We were here, adventure awaited. We were led into the arrivals hall; flies buzzed everywhere, the baggage carousel chugging around squeakily. I could already feel my T-shirt sticking to my back. Then we saw Paul, our guide, holding up a placard saying 'Wild Frontiers'. We headed across to him. He explained that we should get our baggage and follow him. As with most African airports there was a certain ritual to perform to enable us to clear our bags through customs. As we went back to the baggage carousel we checked out our new travelling companions. We had been right, the elderly lady and her daughter, Sarie and Riekie, Afrikaans, and from Pretoria, were part of our group. Then there was Gary and his girlfriend, yuppies from Sandton. An Australian guy and his Mauritian girlfriend completed the group. At long last the arrival formalities were completed and we headed for the truck. As with most rugged overland vehicles it wasn't the most comfortable mode of transport, but it served its purpose.

We headed off to Entebbe Airport Hotel, and were shown to our room. It was basic but clean, sporting a velvety gold and red blanket emblazoned with a lion. A red light permanently on outside the room worried me somewhat, but I convinced myself that it didn't mean anything suggestive! Our meal, as with most meals on the trip, was basic. Peter sampled the local beer for which he developed quite a taste; I tried the local wine, which was sweet and well-nigh undrinkable, although I tried my best to overcome my aversion!

The next day we travelled to Queen Elizabeth National Park, in the Great Lakes region, which promised to be a real treat. We arrived there as the rain clouds started to threaten. Contrary to what it had said in the brochure we *were* expected to erect our own tents. Peter and I had no clue how to do this so we tagged on to Sarie and Riekie, both experienced campers, offering to help them with their tent if they would help us with ours. Of course, they didn't need our help and we were much more of a hindrance to them but they graciously helped us, just finishing in the nick of time before the heavens opened. We retreated into our newly erected shelter to ride out the storm, at least managing to find a bottle of wine and a corkscrew to help us through. By the time Paul came to tell us we could come out, we had become very settled in under the canvas.

Over the next days we saw vast quantities of game at close quarters, hippo, buffalo, elephant, zebra, warthogs and birds aplenty, including fish eagles. It was an unspoilt and remote piece of Africa, a joy to experience.

Peter and I did not endear ourselves to the rest of the group. Uncomfortable with endless group activities, we took ourselves off on our own at every opportunity. We could see the rest of the group couldn't work out our relationship, were we friends or lovers? Peter's spinning convoluted yarns around the campfire, calling me 'Machete Mary' who had killed off several husbands already, didn't help this!

On the fifth day we crossed the border into Rwanda. There was unrest there at the time and we had heard rumours that a group of gorillas had headed into a no-go area in the Democratic Republic of Congo. We had always known that we weren't guaranteed sightings of gorillas but hoped to be lucky. After several hours of wrangling at the border post we made it through to our campsite. Paul gave us strict orders to remain in camp. Naturally, that didn't sit well with us. We knew it was a risk, the town was swarming with soldiers carrying AK-47s, but we felt the need to explore and experience the local culture. We headed out and spent some time in one of the bars and the little shop adjoining it, relishing the chance to practise some French. We had great fun, but were greeted with stony silence when we got back to the camp. We joined the rest of the group for supper and beat a hasty retreat to our tent. We had paid our permits for the next day's trek and had to make an early start from the local parks' office.

We had been told that conditions would be misty and muddy so we wore hiking gear, long pants, a rain jacket and gloves to prevent getting stung by the myriad of nettles in the forest. We arrived at the office and transferred into the back of a clapped-out old bakkie, eight of us, three trackers and four boy soldiers (for protection), armed with AK-47s, and which were held together, somewhat disconcertingly, with bits of Elastoplast and swung around wildly as we careered up the mountain. The situation in the country was volatile and the casual way in which the young soldiers, barely in their teens, handled their weapons made us wonder were they protecting us or did we need protection from them?

The bakkie laboured up the mountain, finally coming to a dead stop at the end of a track. In front of us was dense forest with a bank of mist rolling down the mountain. Our guides explained that they would cut a path through for us, tracking the gorillas from the previous day's sighting. They set off, brandishing machetes, us following, slipping and sliding in the mud. They walked at a brisk pace with us climbing along behind. The air was becoming thinner as we climbed, it was misty but hot, the humidity unbearable beneath our rain jackets. We had hardly begun when Sarie shouted out that Riekie was battling. She was young, quite tubby, but now we realised, clearly unfit. So much for Peter and I going into training for this. Riekie had obviously done nothing to prepare.

Eventually the men pulled her up the mountain using a belt, determined that she should not prevent us seeing the gorillas. We hiked for three hours, slipping and sliding in the mud, holding on to bamboo shoots for balance. It was tough going. Then we came to a clearing where we found the gorillas. We had only half an hour with them. That was the rule, as we are genetically so close to them that we could infect them easily with any of our viruses. We had been instructed not to approach them or make any sudden movements. They looked magnificent in their natural habitat.

Unexpectedly, one of them started to move down the mountain towards us. I moved out of the way but not quickly enough; the gorilla brushed me aside, gently by gorilla standards, but strongly enough to send me reeling. I had felt the warmth of her breath as she lumbered past me and barely managed to keep on my feet, the strength of her slight touch had been so powerful. Peter came rushing over, 'Are you ok, he said, 'I was watching but couldn't do anything to help, she just moved so fast.'

It was an awesome time being with these creatures in such a setting, watching them playing with their babies in the tranquillity of the forest. How lucky I am to have this experience, I thought to myself, it puts so much into perspective. All too soon it was time to leave. We had to trek back down the mountain. The descent was tiring and tricky. I had always battled with downhill stretches and now picking my way gingerly over the bamboo shoots, my mood was not helped by the sight of Riekie, unfit Riekie, hurtling past me on the downhill.

Another two hours down, then a three-hour truck drive to our hotel. It had been a long day but a very special one; we were mucky and tired, looking like we had been dragged through a hedge backwards. I smiled to myself, if John could see me now. He'd never believe I would do a thing like this. How times change. This was something I had done for myself, because I wanted to. I had proved to myself that I could break out of my comfort zone, hike, camp and survive in difficult conditions. It was such an achievement.

Peter grinned at me. 'We made it,' he said, a look of triumph on his face.

Old friends

'Annie loves the photo of you and Peter at the equator,' Kathryn said when I called a couple of weeks later.

We had sent over to her some photos of our trip to the gorillas; she in turn had taken them to Ireland to show to my Aunt Annie. Annie was my father's sister and more like a big sister to Kathryn and myself. She was fourteen years younger than my father, so seemed much closer to our generation, as my parents had had Kathryn and me quite late in life. She had never left Ballinrobe, looking after her mother, my grand-mother, until she died. Annie was great fun, with a wicked sense of humour. When I was a teenager she loved to hear all my stories of going out and the boyfriends I had, starting with Jarlath, the local butcher and my very first boyfriend. She always encouraged me to live life to the full. But when all was said and done, Ballinrobe was a small, conservative Irish town; I wondered what she thought about the John situation. She never mentioned him when we spoke on the phone, but I knew that Kathryn always kept her updated.

'Annie wants to know when you are coming to visit,' Kathryn said. 'She thinks it is about time you came over.'

She was right; I hadn't been over to Ireland for many years. I would generally just visit Kathryn in London and didn't have time to fit in a trip to Ireland. In the last few years going anywhere was impossible as, financially, I had battled. I was starting to get things together though; maybe it was time to go back to my roots. Now that I was working at Gilbeys the extra money coming in helped me pay off my debts. My finances were slowly getting on an even keel.

'I'll think about it,' I replied, 'maybe it could be a possibility.'

I had survived a tough few years both emotionally and financially, battling to service all the debt that John had left me with. I thought the sale of the house in Mondeor would help, only to have the proceeds attached to cover outstanding debts. I hadn't received a cent.

I had cashed up any insurance policies which had a value and left the others to lapse. For some time now the farm had been on the market. I loved it and would miss it, but when I got an offer in early 1996, I just had to accept it. It had been my refuge for so long but I had to do the sensible thing and give it up. It would always have a special place in my heart; my rock had seen me at my most vulnerable and helped me find my way. Now the time had come to move on.

I had struggled to repay the loan on the house I had bought in Regent's Park, which, together with Grotto Bay, took up most of my salary at American Express. Landing the job with Gilbeys had been a godsend. Earning a higher salary gave me the leeway to finish renovations on the Regent's Park house to get it to a reasonable condition for resale. I did the renovations on the cheap, with Nigel, as always, being a willing helper, arranging to sort out the plumbing, sand the floors and generally help me out.

I had managed to sell it with a small profit and could now move to a small townhouse in Winchester Hills. It was newly built, with a view of the Klipriviersberg hills. It felt clean and fresh, a far cry from the Regent's Park house, which, with the best will in the world, would always be dingy and a reminder of how bad things could be. At least here I could have friends round to visit; only a handful of my friends were ever invited to Regent's Park. I knew they would have been horrified and stressed at the thought of me living in such miserable conditions.

My townhouse was not quite ready when I left Regent's Park so my boxes were put into storage. I stayed with Pam for a couple of weeks. The day before the move I went to the townhouse to sleep with just a few clothes and a togbag containing all my precious things that I had not wanted to leave at Pam's: my passport, all the jewellery John had given me through the years and the journals I had kept after he left. I recorded in them the range of emotions I felt as time went by, concern at John's disappearance, anger at his leaving me with so many problems, sadness and hurt at his betrayal of our love.

The builders still had a few finishing touches to make to the townhouse but it was liveable. I spent most of the first evening there cleaning then went to bed exhausted by all my efforts. Stirring in my sleep, I glanced at my watch, 3 a.m. – what was it that had woken me up? I turned over, looked up and stared straight into someone's eyes. A tall man, about six feet, stood in front of me, obviously startled to find me there. He let out a gasp of surprise, picked up my togbag and hotfooted it downstairs. I lay in bed shaking, had he gone? I heard the sound of footsteps running along the paving outside. I got out of bed slowly and looked out of the window, watching him disappear down the road clutching the bag with all my most precious possessions.

My hand shook as I dialled the number for the Flying Squad. They arrived within ten minutes, taking my statement and trying to calm me down. The burglar had got in through one of the windows downstairs, it had been newly glazed and the putty was still soft. I sighed to myself, so much for new beginnings and being safe in my new home. It wasn't the start I was hoping for, or was it? I became philosophical; I had now lost all my connections with the past, the jewellery from John and my record of the last painful years on my own. Maybe this was a sign that I should start looking to the future.

I phoned the office the next morning to tell them what had happened and that I would be a bit late. I had meetings scheduled but only that afternoon and my secretary, Anna, would handle anything that came up. I had lost my air tickets for my trips to Cape Town and Durban the next week, but they would be reissued.

I really enjoyed my new job; I had a lot of responsibility and the autonomy to make things happen. I had to do a lot of travelling around the country but my hard work was starting to reap benefits. My department was reaching and exceeding targets and was being seen as a success story. It was a fast-paced stressful job, but a stimulating one.

'If only John could see you now,' Lynn said to me one day. 'You're quite the executive.'

I smiled, she was right; my life had changed in many ways. I loved what I was doing. It kept me constantly busy and I found myself having less and less time to think of John and what had happened. Financially, I had turned a corner. Laughing, I told her of a phone call I had received the previous day

'Am I speaking to Mrs Monaghan?'

'Yes you are.'

'It is Michael calling from Rand Merchant Bank, we are just transferring your direct debits over to your new account and I wanted to confirm them with you. Have you got a moment?'

I certainly had, it was a pleasure to deal with Rand Merchant Bank. They had approached me to transfer my accounts to them. I felt much less like a number now I qualified to bank with them. It was nice to feel appreciated as a client of theirs and satisfying to think that in a few short years I had gone from almost broke to being approached to be the client of a private bank.

'I'll just confirm the list.' Michael continued, reeling off my insurance debits and car instalments before hesitating, clearly confused: 'Then there is one for SABC, for R19 per month; must this one also be transferred?' I could hear he was curious. Why was I servicing a monthly debit order of just R19 per month? Surely I could pay the annual charge, it would be that much cheaper?

'Yes, please keep it there,' I said, 'It is for my TV licence.'

I had been paying it in monthly instalments since 1993, the year John had gone away. I couldn't manage to pay the full amount of R180 at one go. That would have meant going without food so I arranged for a monthly debit. Now it wouldn't make a dent, I was emotionally attached to this monthly charge, it was a regular reminder of how bad things could be and there was no way I was going to change it. Every month when I saw it on my bank statement it gave me a sense of accomplishment, but also confirmed that things could change and times could be hard again.

'That's it then,' Michael said, 'I'll make sure they are all transferred.'

'That will be great, thanks for your help.' I was glad to get all my accounts sorted out, as I was finally organising a trip overseas to catch up with family and old friends. I had taken Kathryn's advice and knew it was time to go over to Ireland.

I contacted our company travel agent who confirmed that I would be able to get a good deal in June/July, the height of the summer holidays. I knew there would be plenty going on in the town, music concerts, the Ballinrobe Races and many other festivities. Ireland came alive in the summer months. Kathryn would spend all her school holidays in Ireland, so it was also an opportunity for me to spend some time in London on my own, using her flat as my base. I cherished my independence and the thought of a few days visiting galleries and museums on my own was appealing. It might also give me a chance to catch up with some of my school and college friends whom I hadn't seen for years. They always asked me to contact them when I was over in London, but time always seemed too short and most of the holiday was taken up with family obligations.

My trip started to take on epic proportions. I wrote to friends in France and Spain asking if I could visit them. My friend Terry, a professor from the University of Pretoria, was going to be in Paris for a conference and was due to celebrate his fiftieth birthday there. It seemed like an ideal reason to visit Paris and catch up with him and some old friends too. After visiting him I arranged to see my friend Ruth who had studied A-level Spanish with me at Saint Mary's Convent in Cambridge. I was starting to reclaim my life, renewing contact with friends who had been part of it long before John came on the scene.

I also wrote to friends in England, telling them the dates when I would be in London and giving them Kathryn's telephone number. It was hard to believe that it had been almost twenty years since I had seen some of them. Time had just gone by so quickly with all of us tied up with our lives. I was apprehensive about meeting them, what if we had nothing to talk about? I told myself we would find common ground. I had told them about what had happened with John and wanted, in a funny kind of a way, to gain their approval. It seemed right that, now the annulment was through, I made some gesture to kick-start my new life. This was just the opportunity. It would still be some time before I could stop thinking about John and the unanswered questions, which were his legacy to me, yet I felt more in control now. I was less of a victim and more of a survivor with an interesting, if somewhat different, future ahead of me.

I visited Europe before heading off to Ireland. My first stop was Madrid, where my friend Carole met me at the airport. She was just as I remembered her from college. Long blonde hair, blue eyes, she had always been a hit with Spanish men. She was working at a language school there, still not married having been through a series of unsatisfactory relationships. It was great catching up with her again. I spent two hectic days in Madrid. She was working so I spent the days exploring the sights. I passed many hours at the Prado museum; I so loved galleries and museums and missed them in South Africa. In the evenings we experienced the really late nightlife that epitomises Madrid, visiting bars and nightclubs.

My time in Madrid was over all too soon and I took the train to San Sebastian, in Northern Spain, to visit Pilar. She had been a Spanish language assistant in my first year at college, a very religious person, now happily married with teenage children. It was so good to see her again; she hadn't changed and was still as intense and talkative as she had been all those years ago. We revisited our old haunts and caught up on the progress of our lives. I had told her about the annulment and was not sure how she would react, as she was quite conservative, but she told me in no uncertain terms that she considered it the right thing to do. Then it was off to Paris to visit Terry and Ruth.

Paris was all I had remembered it to be, as was Ruth. Only now she was the mother of four young children, so we spent time trying to have a conversation above the racket of four noisy and demanding toddlers.

Then, to the initial reason for me going to Paris, Terry's fiftieth birthday. We celebrated it in great style, taking in a trip on a *bateau-mouche*, dinner at the Eiffel Tower and a show at the Moulin Rouge. It was good to be extravagant again, having scrimped and saved for so long.

Next stop Ireland. I was excited about seeing Annie again. I had always been very close to her but was unsure how things would be. Would she disapprove of what I had done? Would she judge me harshly? Obtaining her approval would, by default, be gaining the approval of my parents.

She and Kathryn met me at Knock airport on a warm summer's afternoon. It was about a forty-five minute drive to Ballinrobe and we spent the time discussing my trip to France and Spain. Ballinrobe was the closest place to home I had. Both my parents had been born and raised in Ballinrobe, my mother from High Street and my father from Glebe Street. It had been the one constant in my life. I got out of the car in front of Annie's house. As I breathed in the unmistakeable, lingering scent of turf fires, I felt safe.

We sat down at the kitchen table while Annie bustled around making us tea and coffee. Eventually she sat down too, 'Show me your ring,' she said, pulling my hand towards her.

I had moved my wedding ring to my right hand and had replaced it with my Claddagh ring. She knew well that the Claddagh ring, originating as it did from the West of Ireland, had a particular significance depending which way round it was worn. If the crown closed the heart you were unavailable but if the heart was open you were single. Its significance was understood in Ireland, but I bemoaned the fact that its symbolism was unrecognised in South Africa. No chance of meeting a man by showing him my availability via a ring!

I gave Annie my hand, smiling sheepishly.

'Good,' she said as she recognised I was showing myself to be available, 'that's how it should be.'

Nothing further was said on the subject, the matter was closed but she had voiced her approval. I felt as if a great weight had lifted from my soul. I had done the right thing, and nobody thought the worse of me for it. The annulment was accepted so easily by everyone that I encountered in Ireland that I questioned why I had made such a big deal of it, maybe it had all been in my mind. I realised that it had been many years since I had visited Ireland and in that time the people and the Church had become far more progressive and forgiving. I had been visualising the rigid Church of twenty years ago and was unaware that it and the people had moved on.

My holiday in Ireland was happy and carefree. Of course, I still thought of John, Ireland was his home too and I knew he would have loved the music and the atmosphere so much. Although I had never lived in Ireland, I was surrounded by family who cared for me. I no longer had to pretend that I was coping; there were friends and family to support me. I realised that the lack of family in South Africa had been one of the hardest things for me after John's disappearance. I always gave the impression of being strong and coping but deep down I was fragile and broken, barely having the strength to get through each day. It would have been so much better if I had had someone to hold me and say, 'Don't worry it will be all right. We're here for you'. Now, in Ballinrobe I had all the support I could wish for and revelled in it.

All too soon it was time to go back to London. I was hoping to catch up with some more of my school and college friends. Maybe I would have a few messages when I got to Kathryn's flat. What if no one had phoned? I thought. I let myself into the flat in Cricklewood to be greeted by the flashing light of the answering machine. It looked as if there were several messages. All the friends I had written to had phoned. I made arrangements to meet them in London, several of them travelling far to spend just a few hours with me. I felt so special; to think they were all willing to make such an effort was flattering. The entire trip had made me feel so loved and cared for. Why had I waited so long to catch up with them?

There was just one more special person I had to contact, Father Joe. I always visited him when I was in London and he too knew what had happened with John. I had written to tell him about the divorce and the annulment. What would he think? He was quite old now and probably very conservative, but it was important to me that he approved of what I had done.

We arranged to meet at Tottenham Court Road tube and went to Garfunkel's Restaurant (our usual haunt). We had been meeting there on and off for the last ten years. Father Joe was a link to my parents and I tried to see him each time I visited London. He was based at a parish in Clerkenwell and would walk to Tottenham Court Road easily from there. Garfunkel's was a convenient spot to rendezvous for a drink and a meal. I was nervous, I didn't know how to broach the subject of the annulment, it was just too embarrassing. I needn't have worried. We had barely settled into our seats when he looked at me and said: 'John was a fool to leave a great girl like you. I'm glad you've put it behind you.'

'Thank you,' I said, trying to hold back the tears.

'You've done the right thing,' he continued.

I smiled shakily. 'Do you really think so?'

'Of course, now what shall we order?'

I sighed quietly; this was the last approval I needed. I didn't have to justify what I had done to anyone else; all the important people in my life had supported my decision. I was free to move on at last. My trip had served its purpose. I had revisited my roots and started to reclaim my life, at its very beginning point. I had turned the corner.

Granny's funeral

'Did I wake you up?' Kathryn asked.

It was 9.30 p.m. one September evening in 1997 and she knew that was quite late to phone me on a weeknight. Of course, in London, it was only 8.30 p.m., still early for her.

'No, it's fine, I've just got out of the bath, I wasn't going to go to bed for a little while yet.'

'I've just had a phone call from Elizabeth,' she said.

Elizabeth, the aunt who was more like a big sister to John than the aunt she was, had often joined us on nights out at the Tara Club in Harlesden when we lived in London all those years ago. She had been a good friend to me after John had gone away, phoning me regularly at Christmas and New Year to see how I was coping. Now she had her own troubles. She had phoned Kathryn to say that her mother, John's grandmother, had died. 'Granny', as family and friends alike affectionately knew her, had been like a mother to John. It was to her that he had gone when, at the age of seventeen, he had left home and moved to London to make a life for himself. A strong no-nonsense woman from County Donegal, she had a heart of gold and made an impression on everyone she met.

'The funeral is on Wednesday afternoon,' Kathryn continued. 'I'm going to go. What should I tell them?'

I had finalised my divorce and annulment a few months earlier, but had not told any of John's family. What difference did it make, when all was said and done?

'Should I tell them?' she asked.

'Go ahead,' I responded, 'it's no big deal, it's not as if they can tell John anyway.'

'I just wanted to be sure, I'd hate to put my foot in it.'

Kathryn phoned me again on the Wednesday evening after the funeral, 'They had a great day for it, dry and sunny, and there was a good turn out. I spoke to John and Maisie and Elizabeth,' she said. 'It was a bit strange though, Elizabeth took me to one side and said she had to talk to me but couldn't do it there and she would phone me. I'm sure she'll give me a call soon. I wonder what it is about?'

I wondered, too. John had been gone for almost five years now. Could she possibly have news of him? I doubted it. I'd had so many false hopes raised. I wasn't even going to think like that. Each time I had a call from a private investigator saying they had found someone only to find that it was a short, balding, fifty-five year old with no resemblance to John. I had obtained three Australian visas in the last five years, believing that I was close to finding him each time, only to have my hopes dashed every time. I had refused to give up my search for him.

'Let me know as soon as she contacts you,' I said to Kathryn.

'You know I will.'

Days went by and I heard nothing. Finally, I phoned Kathryn.

'You just caught me,' she said. ' I was on my way out to music.'

'Have you heard from Elizabeth?'

'Not a word. I've tried to phone her a couple of times but there was no answer.'

'Don't worry, I'll phone, maybe I'll be lucky. I'll keep you posted.'

I took a deep breath; I just had to find out what she wanted. It could be something or nothing for that matter, either way I had to find out.

A phone call to Elizabeth was always stressful. She cared so much about me, but every time we spoke she insisted on revisiting the past and exclaiming as she went on at the unfairness of it all. I settled myself into my armchair, wrapped up in my warm towelling gown. I'd just had a hot steamy bath in calming aromatherapy oils. The sound of my Mary Black CD played softly in the background. I was ready for this phone call, whatever it would reveal.

I dialled the number, it rang several times. 'Please let her be there,' I said to myself. Just as I was about to give up, Elizabeth answered.

'Hello it's Mary from Johannesburg,' I said to her. 'I was so sorry to hear about Granny.' I had been very upset by the news of her death, especially, as I knew how much she had meant to John and I was saddened at the thought that I couldn't even tell him that she was dead. I knew he would be devastated, she had meant so much to him.

'How are you doing?' I asked

'I'm ok. The house seems very empty without her; there are so many reminders of her around the place.'

'I know,' I said, 'it's not easy; it will take time to come to terms with it.'

'It was so good of Kathryn to come to the funeral, it meant a lot to us.'

'She wanted to be there on my behalf too,' I replied; 'Granny was a very special person.'

'I meant to phone Kathryn,' Elizabeth replied 'but I didn't get round to it.'

'She did mention it,' I responded, hoping that now Elizabeth would tell me whatever had been on her mind.

'This is very difficult,' she said. 'I promised John's mother that I wouldn't tell, but I have to, it's only fair. Something happened a few months ago in the summer. We've had contact with John.'

And nobody told me! I wanted to scream at her. That was the agreement, whoever heard had promised to tell the other. When John had first gone away, his mother had written to me from time to time, checking if I had heard anything:

Mary, have you heard anything of John? It's very lonely not knowing where he is especially at Christmas.

It must be very hard on you not knowing where he is. He seems to have forgotten any of us exist. Let's hope he is safe and well wherever he is.

To be fair, she had written to me in 1996, after a distant relative had run into him in Australia:

A friend of hers came into contact with John, he must have said something about Ireland. It seems when she said who she knew, he didn't want to know. She said he had a girl with him Mary. It's sad to say but you Mary go ahead with the annulment and make a life for yourself.

'John's mother was worried that he would be cross if I told you,' she said. 'But let me tell you what happened, it's a long story:

'Three months ago in August, John's mother, Margaret, received a call from an Australian woman, Mrs Smith. Margaret had just been in the field with the cows and as she got back into the house the phone rang. The Australian woman on the other end of the phone said that Margaret would not know her, but she was visiting Ireland on business. She had finished her official business now and had added a few extra days to her trip to attend to some personal matters.'

Elizabeth continued, somewhat relaxing into her story, 'This is what she said to Margaret: "My daughter is involved with someone in Sydney, he's Irish and comes from Cashelard, and his name is John Monaghan. I think he may be your son."

'Margaret couldn't believe what she was hearing, it could be John.

'Mrs Smith asked if she could come to visit, she was only a few miles away and would like to talk to Margaret in person. Of course, she was welcome; it had been so long since John had gone away and now finally they would have some news. Margaret gave the woman directions to their farm just outside Ballyshannon in County Donegal. She was on her own that afternoon, as John's father had gone to town to do some errands.

'Just half an hour later a car pulled up at the door and a large imposing woman got out. She was about the same age as Margaret with a businesslike, no-nonsense air about her.

'They sipped tea together, and eventually after the small talk was out of the way, Mrs Smith told Margaret her story:

"My daughter is seeing someone called John Monaghan. They have been together for a few years now and he is always very secretive about his past, but through the years I have gathered some information, which has led me here. He mentioned that he grew up on a farm in Cashelard, and that he worked in London and then went to South Africa before coming to Australia, but I know there are things he is not telling me. Neither he nor my daughter knows I am here and I do not intend to tell them when I get back, but I just need to know for my own piece of mind.'''

'Margaret was overcome,' Elizabeth said. 'She told me she could hardly speak, it was so unexpected for her to hear news of John. She told her about you and your life together in South Africa, how he had vanished and the difficult time which you had been through. She said she even showed her your wedding photo, still proudly displayed on the mantelpiece. Apparently Mrs Smith wasn't surprised.

"I just knew there was something," she said to Margaret. "I'm so sorry you have all been so worried. I don't want him to think I have interfered so I won't tell him of my visit, but if you ever need to contact him urgently, I'll give you my contact details and I will pass on a message for you."'''

'Margaret ran to the bedroom to fetch a pen and paper. She talked a little more to Mrs Smith and then saw her to her car as she prepared to leave.'

'Margaret phoned me later that evening,' Elizabeth continued. 'She made me promise not to tell you, she was worried what you might do with the information, saying blood is thicker than water after all.'

I struggled to hold back the tears as Elizabeth recounted the story, kicking against the unfairness of it all.

'But that's not all,' she continued.

I settled back in my chair, steeling myself for the next onslaught. I was already feeling battered and bruised.

'Granny became sick,' Elizabeth continued, 'so Margaret decided to contact Mrs Smith and take the risk of angering John by telling him of her trip to Ireland, just hoping that he would forgive her interference, knowing how much Granny meant to him.'

'She managed to get a message to John just in time for him to phone Granny in hospital before she died. He didn't make it over for her funeral but sent flowers.'

An overwhelming sense of anger came over me. All this time I had been upset that John didn't know that Granny had died and he knew. Not only did he know, he spoke to her on her deathbed. His family knew where he was and they hadn't even let me know.

I sobbed into the phone, 'It's just so unfair. All this time I have been looking for John and I have found nothing but dead ends. Now, in a way, John has found his family through Mrs Smith and they haven't even told me. I'm sorry if I sound cross, but I can't help it. It's just all too much.'

'I know,' Elizabeth said. 'It's very hard but Margaret wouldn't even tell me where he was in case I told you. No-one else knows, she's so worried he would be cross with her for telling you, even John and Maisie don't know.'

'Why would he be cross? I've done nothing wrong.'

I couldn't believe the injustice of it all. It was great to hear news of him but now I still couldn't speak to him. I pulled yet another tissue out of the box I had strategically placed close to the chair, knowing I would need them, but having no idea just how much.

Elizabeth's voice was soothing on the other end of the line, trying to calm me. 'I promise I'll get details for you, I will. Don't worry.'

I knew she realised how important it was for me and I didn't doubt for a moment she would help me. There was nothing more to say, I needed to get off the phone and come to terms with what I had just heard. There were just too many thoughts racing through my head. I needed to slow myself down and deal with them rationally.

'Thanks Elizabeth, I know you didn't have to tell me. I know it's not your fault, but I really need to find John, it's just so frustrating.'

'I know, I know, I'll get the information. Take care. I'll speak to you soon.'

I dropped the receiver back into the cradle, leaned back in the chair and let the tears flow, tears of relief, anger and helplessness. So near and yet so far, how much longer would this go on?

Journey's end

Weeks turned into months and soon it was over a year since the phone call with Elizabeth had revealed that John's family had made contact with him. I phoned Elizabeth several times; unable to comprehend that she had not been able to find his details. Each time she was full of apologies but confirmed that no progress had been made.

I resigned myself to the fact that I was unlikely ever to find John. It was incredible but once again my hopes had been dashed. I just couldn't understand why I was battling so much, how difficult could it be? It was pointless trying to contact his mother; Elizabeth had made me promise that I wouldn't tell Margaret that she had told me. I just couldn't bring myself to break my promise to her.

'Guess who left a message on my answering machine last night?' I said to Deirdre as I arrived at work on a beautiful summer's morning in December 1998.

I had known Deirdre since I had taken over the running of the Customer Service section of Nedbank Card Division, on the Visa/MasterCard side. She was younger than me, a bubbly, no-nonsense person with a passion for customer service and a work ethic second to none. She had reported to me for several years, meeting me after John had already left for Australia and joining me later at Gilbeys. We became firm friends and would often play squash together or go for spinning classes.

'Elizabeth?'

'How did you guess?'

'What did she want?'

'I don't know. I was out when she phoned. I'll try and catch her tonight. I want to get hold of her as soon as possible. A phone call with her is always unsettling, so the sooner I get it over and done with the better. I can't believe it is over a year since she promised to get John's number and still I've heard nothing. I don't think she has any idea just how stressful and frustrating this is for me.'

I still hadn't managed to take Elizabeth's phone calls in my stride; she always upset me. This time I was determined to have the upper hand and speak to her when it suited me. Each time she phoned I thought that maybe this time I would be given some way of contacting John. Still she hadn't managed to get me a contact number for him.

That night I prepared myself for the phone call just as before. It was becoming a ritual for me. First of all a hot, scented bath full of relaxing aromatherapy oils, soft candlelight in the bathroom, then, warmly wrapped in my towelling dressing gown I would sit in my favourite chair. Soft Irish music playing in the background, a box of tissues to my side, I would dial the number.

Why am I making such a big thing of this? I thought to myself, it won't be any different to every other time; she'll have no real news. The phone continued to ring on the other side, she should be at home. It must be about 8 p.m. in England now.

At last she answered the phone breathlessly, 'You've just caught me,' she said. 'I was at our company's Christmas lunch and have just got in.'

You could tell that she had had a few glasses of wine, her speech was slightly slurred. We talked easily; she was always interested in how I was doing and what was happening in my life. She hoped to win the lottery so that she could come to visit me in South Africa. As usual she started to rehash the past: 'You seemed so happy together; I can't believe that he left. Why did he not contact you again? He really is very bad. You didn't deserve this.'

'I can't believe you never managed to find his number for me,' I retorted, my patience wearing thin. It was all very well being sympathetic but didn't Elizabeth realise that the best thing she could have done to help me was to find John's address? Things went from bad to worse when she decided to tell me that John had been over to Ireland on holiday. She told me that his mother had remained loyal to me and mentioned my name to him at every opportunity when he was visiting. I sighed to myself. This really wasn't helping.

'I found John in the front room one day,' she continued, 'he didn't realise I was watching him. He was looking at your wedding photo with tears in his eyes.'

Great, that's doing me the world of good, I thought. I felt like shaking her. 'So why didn't you speak up?' I asked.

'I didn't have a chance to speak to him alone. His girlfriend was always with him. I didn't manage to catch him on his own.'

Tears of helplessness streamed down my cheeks.

'He's put on weight you know, you probably wouldn't recognise him. He's not looking as good as when you last saw him,' she prattled on.

I couldn't believe her insensitivity, but it was done unconsciously and not meaning any harm.

I repeated, 'I can't believe you couldn't find a number for him.'

'You're right,' she said. 'I should have been able to find something.'

We were now a good forty-five minutes into the phone call. The music had long since stopped and still we were going around in circles.

'Hold on a minute,' she said. 'Maybe I do have something. They sent flowers for the funeral last year; perhaps I've still got the card. I'll look in Granny's room. I've only been in there twice since she died. Hold on.'

I gulped. Maybe she had something, but I doubted it. Almost six years of false alarms meant that I didn't let my hopes get raised unnecessarily.

'I've found something,' she said, 'a card, there's a phone number on it.'

Probably a false one, I thought to myself, sceptical to the last.

'Have you got a pen? I'll read it to you.'

'Just a minute, I'll get one.' I rushed to my handbag to find one; it was taking too long, and I tipped the contents out all over the floor. At last I found one. My heart started to race. Could this really be it?

She read the number to me. 'Will you phone?' she asked.

'Maybe,' I said nonchalantly. I was starting to get the feeling that she doubted she had done the right thing. 'It's probably a false number,' I said trying to play the whole thing down.

'Can you believe I've had it all this time?' she said guilelessly.

I finished the conversation as quickly as possible. I just had to try the number. Elizabeth carried on talking, but eventually I got a word in and we said our goodbyes.

I took a deep breath, nervous but still convinced this was yet another false lead. I tapped out the number. The phone rang. So this is a valid number, my heart was thumping, what was I going to say? After all this time, I wasn't prepared for this.

No answer. The call linked into an answering machine. 'Hi, you have reached John and Tamsin,' a woman's voice said. 'We're not able to take your call now but please leave a message.'

I hurriedly dropped the phone, hardly believing my ears. I had the right number. I looked at my watch trying to calculate the time in Australia. It's the middle of the night there, I thought, no wonder they didn't answer. What if in Australia they take their summer holidays over Christmas? They could be away for weeks. I might not be able to speak to him for ages. I was still remarkably calm, not truly believing that I had got so close. It seemed unbelievable after all these years, as if it was happening in slow motion.

I'll just have to try again in the morning, I thought to myself as I got into bed where I fell into a deep sleep. The alarm was set for 5 a.m. to give me time to phone before leaving for work. Christmas time was our peak season and I had the keys to the office and needed to be there at 7 a.m. to let the staff in. I leaned out of the bed and reached for the phone, grabbing the piece of paper on which I had written John's number. I dialled once more; convinced I would link into the answering machine again. The phone rang a few times and then John answered. I couldn't believe my ears; I battled to stop the tears flowing, gulping hard.

Speak, I said to myself, now's your moment. I had thought about this for years. I had played so many scenarios out in my mind, but now I felt totally unprepared.

'Hello,' I said shakily. 'Remember me? This is a voice from your past.'

'Of course I do,' he responded quietly. The line was bad, it was obviously a cell phone connection, it crackled, echoed and then went dead. His voice sounded no different to the tape I used to play every birthday.

I sat with the phone in my hand, tears streaming down my face. I'd spoken to John, but now what? Had he put down the phone or had we really lost the connection? I tried again; it went straight onto voice mail. I tried on and off five or six times, I couldn't believe it, surely he hadn't switched his phone off, he wouldn't be so heartless?

I started to get ready for work. I'll try one last time before I leave, I said to myself, preparing to get irritated once more by the sound of his message. This time it rang, but it wasn't John who answered, it was a woman.

'I'd like to speak to John please,' I said imperiously, no one was going to get the better of me at this point.

'He's at the doctor's surgery,' she replied.

'Please ask him to phone Mary. I'll give you my number.' I repeated it carefully to her. 'Will he phone back?' I asked.

'I don't know,' she responded.

Luckily I could divert my landline to my cell phone. I didn't relish the thought of him catching me on my way to the office, while I was driving, but there was very little I could do. What if he didn't phone back? I couldn't believe he would do that to me, but then how well did I really know him? The last few years had proved that. If he didn't phone me back that day I was determined to leave a message for him, saying that I would deal with him face to face if not telephonically, it was his choice.

I locked the townhouse, drove the car out of the garage, took a deep breath and set off to work, my cell phone close to me on the passenger seat. It was light, a beautiful Highveld summer's day. I put the radio on, anything to distract me as I willed my phone to ring. Concentrate, I kept telling myself. Keep your eyes on the road, watch what you are doing.

I arrived at work in a daze, parked in my usual parking bay. As I unlocked the office, some of the staff were already there waiting for me. I'm not sure if they noticed the wild look in my eyes. I greeted them as usual and headed for the sanctuary of my own office. At least here I can have some privacy I said to myself, as I closed the blinds, put my extension on 'do not disturb' and placed the key in the lock at the back of the door. If he phones me now, I won't be disturbed I thought.

I prowled around the office, pacing up and down like a caged animal. I walked for stress, but somehow today it wasn't helping to calm me down. He just had to phone.

I prayed quietly, please God help me, I just need to speak to him.

Through the window I watched the traffic on the highway, it all looked so normal. Did nobody realise what I was going through? I adjusted my skirt; I looked a bit dishevelled. I had flung my clothes on in such a hurry, totally distracted.

At long last the phone rang.

'Mary Monaghan speaking,' I answered.

'Hallo,' John responded. 'You didn't deserve what I did to you,' he said, his voice low and full of emotion.

I felt the tears well up, keep calm I said to myself, don't waste this moment. 'I know I didn't deserve it,' my voice was shaky and tearful.

'I never meant to hurt you.'

'But you did.'

'I know.'

Our conversation was loving and tender. Finally, I had the chance to ask all the unanswered questions that had plagued me for almost six years.

'Did you mean to come back?'

'Yes.'

'Was there something I could have done?'

'No.'

'Did you mean to hurt me?'

'No, I never meant to hurt you; you know I wouldn't want to do that. It's complicated, it just happened, I never intended it to work out like this.'

'Why didn't you contact me and tell me what was going on?'

'I meant to and then too much time had gone by, it seemed too late. I'm sorry, I know what I did was wrong, I know it must have been difficult for you.'

'You have no idea, so much has happened,' I struggled to fight back the tears. I need to talk to John, I thought, I can't choke on the words.

'Are things ok with you now?'

'Yes, my life has come together. My friends have been great.'

'I shouldn't have done what I did. You deserved better than this.'

I felt vindicated. I had maintained this all along, but no one believed me. I knew what John had done was wrong and unforgivable, but he hadn't done it intentionally and with malice. I still felt hurt and betrayed though.

Our conversation continued, both of us battling through the emotion of the situation. We weren't prepared, so we hopped from one topic to the other, talking of mundane things one minute and painful emotions the next. At last the call drew to a close.

'I know I need to explain,' he said. 'You deserve at least that. I'll phone or write soon and we can go over everything when we are calmer. I promise I'll be in touch soon and explain what happened.'

I smiled to myself, it was the conversation that I had visualised for so long, and it was gentle, tender and loving. I was saddened but content at the same time. 'Goodbye,' I said as I hung up.

I glanced at my watch. We had been talking for nearly an hour. Now the tears flowed freely as I continued pacing around the small office, talking aloud to myself, saying: 'I don't believe it, I don't believe it.'

I knew I needed to get out to walk off the emotion and compose myself. I must look a sight, I thought, but I need to get out. I dried the tears from my face, put on my sunglasses and prepared to bolt, past the staff sitting outside my office, towards reception and the outside world. They were all busy on the phone. I hurried past them, saying, 'I'll be back soon', to no one in particular as I headed off to walk around the office complex. No one walked there, but I needed to. I wandered aimlessly up and down the closes. Thembi, one of my staff, waved at me from her Toyota Venture, 'You're going the wrong way.'

'I know, I'll see you soon,' I responded.

An hour later I made my way back to the office, heading straight for my desk, acknowledging no one. I closed the door, sat down and took a deep breath. There was a tentative knock at the door.

'Who is it?'

'Deirdre. We've been worried about you.'

I let her in.

'We saw your car downstairs, your blinds were closed, your office door was locked and your phone was on 'do not disturb'. We were worried about you.'

She took one look at me. My face said it all.

'What happened? Did you get to speak to Elizabeth?'

The story tumbled out. Tears welled in her eyes to match mine. She was devastated. 'Are you all right?'

'Yes I am. I truly am. I feel settled; I've finally found answers to my questions.' It was true; it had been traumatic, but also settling in a funny kind of way. Not quite an anticlimax, but a closure. There were so many people to tell and it was such a long story, but they all needed to know. It was going to be a long day.

'Don't worry about going to Gino's tonight for dinner,' she said.

'Of course we'll go,' I replied. 'It will be a celebration. I wouldn't miss it for the world.' I needed to break out after the release from all those years of pent up emotion.

I knew I needed to tell all my friends, it was such a long saga though, each call would last ages. So many of my friends had already gone away for the Christmas holidays. I knew I wouldn't be able to reach all of them and didn't want to interfere with their break.

I had to start with Nigel; he deserved to be told first. He had been such a special friend to me through the years.

'Hi Nigel, how are you? Where are you?'

'In the shop.'

'Good, are you sitting down?'

'Why?'

'Guess who I spoke to today?'

'Not John?'

'Oh yes.'

'You're kidding'

I told him the whole story, he knew how many false alarms I had had until then, so he was more than aware of the significance of what had just happened.

'Are you all right? You must give me his number; I need to tell him what I think about him. Who does he think he is? I hope he apologised at least.'

I told Nigel that John was going to contact me again and I asked him to be patient and wait until after that. I wanted to handle it my way first.

By that evening I'd told almost everyone I needed to. It was exhausting, there was so much they wanted to know but I had to speak to them all, they deserved it. It was interesting to see the difference in reactions between my male and female friends. My female friends were very supportive and understood when I said I had had a good conversation with John. The men on the other hand were angry and outraged at what John had done to me and couldn't understand why I hadn't got cross with him and given him hell. I didn't need to. I knew the guilt of what he had done would always haunt him.

I was just glad I had spoken to him; I felt an overwhelming sense of calm. No matter what he had done to me it was still good to speak to him. As Wendy had said to me a year or so before: 'Cross as I am at what he did to you, I'd still love to see him again. It's hard to stay angry with him.' I knew what she meant; John was a charmer who had done a really cruel and hurtful thing. I could forgive that, but I would never forget.

Apart from the first Christmas when John had gone away and I had expected him to fly in at any moment, I had continued with the tradition of cooking Christmas lunch and surrounding myself with friends. For some reason this year I had planned things differently. I had received invitations from so many friends. Just as well, I would not have been able to concentrate on Christmas arrangements considering the drama unfolding in my life.

The day after speaking to John was Christmas Eve and I had arranged to take a cooked turkey through to Pretoria to my friend Terry who was having a party for his students. I couldn't let him down, so managed to do this in the midst of the excitement. I arrived at his house that evening, my car full of roses bought for me by my colleagues. They were in buckets on the floor of the car; there must have been at least five dozen of them. It was their way of showing that they knew what had happened and that they understood and wanted to show me how much they cared. I was really touched by their gesture.

Terry couldn't believe it: 'They must think a lot of you,' he said.

'I think so,' I replied, trying to contain my emotions.

On Christmas morning I went to Braamfontein to Mass as I always did and lit a candle of thanks for finding John. It was a special Christmas Day, my heart full of emotion as I allowed myself to wallow in the sentimentality of the Christmas carols.

'Come in, come in,' Helga said as I arrived on her doorstep after Mass. Helga had never been the most demonstrative of people, but today she hugged me tight with tears in her eyes. 'Are you all right?' she asked.

'Of course,' I replied, tears rolling down my cheeks. 'I am, I really am, I'm emotional but fine.'

She busied herself in the kitchen, getting out two champagne glasses to accompany our brunch. We toasted each other, drinking to the future.

Then it was off to Peter's family for lunch in Bryanston. In true Greek fashion they had invited lots of family for the occasion. It was a noisy, festive time. Lunch lasted for ages, as course after course came out of the kitchen. The food was outstanding, wine flowed freely and conversations were noisy and intense. I was made to feel truly welcome as I was introduced to every last cousin there that day. It was just what I needed, lots of hustle and bustle and a great feeling of being loved and cared for.

There was still another stop to make. Peter and I left to visit Wendy and her family in the late afternoon. They were relaxing outside on the stoep, recovering from the excesses of Christmas lunch. I wanted to get Wendy on her own to tell her about John, but it was easier said than done as one or other member of her family kept demanding her attention. At long last we retreated to her bedroom and I started to tell her the news. She wanted to know everything, so I gave her a blow-by-blow account of John's and my conversation.

'Did you tell him about the divorce and annulment?' she asked. As she had been interviewed during the annulment process, she was interested to know.

'No, I didn't, it was too emotional. We didn't talk about those admin kind of things. I'll tell him when he contacts me again and we are more prepared.'

'You're right,' she said, 'it'll be easier to discuss next time you speak to him.'

'Would you think about taking him back?' Wendy was never frightened to ask the questions other people were too afraid to ask.

'No, I wouldn't. Too much has happened. I could never trust him again.'

'Do you still love him?'

'Of course I do, I will never stop loving him, but I could never be with him again.'

'You're right, I know what you mean, too much has changed. I can't believe you finally found him. You look fine. Are you sure you're all right?'

I assured her I was, it was so great to be able to tell people about John, I was revelling in it. I felt strong and in control, almost triumphant. I had found John as I said I would and had discovered the answers to the questions that had plagued me since his disappearance. I could just imagine how he was feeling this Christmas, but I felt all right.

In the days and weeks that followed I waited patiently for the phone to ring or a letter to arrive. John had promised to contact me again, to give me more answers and explanations about why he had done what he had done. He had promised, surely he wouldn't break *this* promise? I had told Nigel I wouldn't give him the phone number until I had heard from John again, but how much longer should I wait before giving it to him?

Four months went by and still no word. I couldn't believe John's absolute insensitivity. He had already done such damage and was doing nothing to make things better. Eventually I phoned Nigel to give him the number.

'Don't worry,' he said, 'he doesn't deserve to be phoned. I really don't want to speak to him.'

I have not heard from John again, although another seven years have passed. My anger at his final act of selfishness soon abated. What purpose would further contact serve anyway? My life continued at its usual busy pace, with me working hard, pursuing my career and surrounding myself with wonderful friends. I realised he no longer had a place in my life.

I gazed at the reds and oranges of the sunset as I sat at last on the stoep of my little house by the sea and reflected on the woman I had become. The woman who had phoned John was not the woman he had left behind. I was a strong, independent and fulfilled woman, not the vulnerable, needy wife he once knew.

'Remember me?' No you don't. The woman you remember no longer exists.

Mary Monaghan's roots are in Ireland. In South Africa she divides her time between Grotto Bay and Cape Town. She has a wide range of interests, both personal and commercial. She writes, learns new languages, travels extensively and spends time with friends and family.